Dedicated to
Ben Gilman and Fred Tuckman

David

Poet, warrior, king

Fred Catherwood

Inter-Varsity Press

INTER-VARSITY PRESS
38 De Montfort Street, Leicester LE1 7GP, England

Unless otherwise stated, Scripture quotations in this publication are from
the Holy Bible, New International Version. Copyright © 1973, 1978, 1984
International Bible Society. Published in Great Britain by Hodder and
Stoughton Ltd.

First published 1993

British Library Cataloguing in Publication Data
A catalogue record for this book is available from the British Library.

ISBN 0-85110-863-6

Set in Palacio
Typeset in Great Britain by Avocet Typesetters, Bicester, Oxon.
Printed and bound in Great Britain by Cox & Wyman Ltd, Reading Berks.

*Inter-Varsity Press is the book-publishing division of the Universities and Colleges
Christian Fellowship (formerly the Inter-Varsity Fellowship), a student movement
linking Christian Unions in universities and colleges throughout the United Kingdom
and the Republic of Ireland, and a member movement of the International Fellowship
of Evangelical Students. For information about local and national activities write to
UCCF, 38 De Montfort Street, Leicester LE1 7GP.*

Contents

List of maps

Preface

As I was writing this extraordinary story of the legendary King David, the names on the TV news were just the same as the names in the story of his reign three thousand years ago. A state of Israel, occupied again by the same people in lineal descent, had made peace with Egypt. The modern Ammonites, however, in their present capital of Amman, were hostile, as were the Syrians in the north, still in their old capital of Damascus. The Lebanese merchants of Tyre and Sidon still preferred trade to war, if they could have it. Farther south, Gaza, the heartland of the Philistines, was occupied by Israel but still restless and resentful. David's city of Jerusalem was again the seat of government and the strategic objectives of the Israeli army seemed roughly the same as those of David, when he had to hold his own against the same encircling enemies.

David is more than a king who lived and died three thousand years ago. He is more even than a symbol to a scattered people who have, miraculously, survived as a race for all of that time. His name is bound up with the promise of a messianic figure who, some believe, is still to come in order to secure Israel once and for all in its former territories. That view is not confined to Zionists; it is also held by a majority of fundamentalist Christians in the United States. Their belief has been a constant political factor in American encouragement to the formation and build-up of the present state of Israel. So I have felt that, in addition to the story of David, this book should examine the messianic promises.

As one engaged in the great attempt to find ways of binding the twelve warring tribes of Western Europe into a peaceful confederation, I have found a study of David's success in binding – and keeping – the twelve tribes of Israel together very helpful. His patience, especially, is a lesson for us as he faced the instinctive separatism of 'To your tents, O Israel!'; a call which has a very contemporary ring!

I have tried to write the historical chapters as fact rather than as 'faction', the mixture of fact and fiction, which is neither one thing nor the other. But even the bare bones of the story, as told in the books of Samuel and Chronicles, carries its own excitement, and I hope that the reader will enjoy reading it as much as I have enjoyed writing it.

Fred Catherwood
Cambridge
Summer 1992

Dramatis Personae

Abiathar Son of Ahimelech and his successor as priest.

Abigail Wife and then widow of Nabal, a wise woman and David's third wife, who bore him a second son, Kileab.

Abishag Wife and companion to David in the last years.

Abishai Brother of Joab and a leader in his army.

Abner Cousin of King Saul and commander of his army.

Absalom David's third son, born to Maacah, daughter of Talmai, King of Geshur; leader of an unsuccessful rebellion against his father.

Achish King of Gath, one of the kings of the Philistines who befriended David in his exile.

Adonijah David's fourth son, born to Haggith, who conspired unsuccessfully against Solomon's successor.

Ahimaaz Son of Zadok the priest.

Ahimelech Priest of Israel, descended through the line of high priests from Aaron, brother of Moses, Israel's first high priest: murdered with all his family on Saul's orders.

Ahitophel David's counsellor, who deserted him for Absalom and subsequently committed suicide.

Amasa Captain of Absalom's forces.

Amnon David's eldest son, born to his second wife, Ahinoam of Jezreel.

Araunah A Jebusite, owner of the threshing floor which was sold to David for an altar and on which the temple was built.

Asahel Brother of Joab and a brave officer in his army.

Bathsheba Uriah's wife and widow; married to David and mother of Solomon, David's successor.

Beniah Son of Jehoida, captain of the king's guard.

David Youngest son of Jesse of Bethlehem of the clan of Judah, shepherd, poet, musician, warrior, outlaw and King of Judah and Israel, the subject of this history.

Gad A prophet, David's adviser.

Goliath A giant of a man from Gath, champion of the Philistines, Israel's enemies.

Hushai David's friend.

Ish-Bosheth A surviving son of Saul and his immediate successor, as king of the northern clans.

Joab Son of David's sister, Zeruiah, and head of David's army.

Jonathan Son of Abiathar the priest.

Jonathan Son of King Saul, a brave soldier and leader and a close friend of David.

Kileab David's second son, born to the wise Abigail.

Mephibosheth A cripple, son of Jonathan and grandson of King Saul.

Michal Second daughter of King Saul, David's first wife, who was childless.

Nathan A prophet and spiritual adviser to David.

Samuel A prophet and the last of the line of the judges who ruled Israel between the conquest of the land of Canaan and the anointing of Saul as Israel's first king.

Saul First king of the nation of Israel, son of Kish of the clan of Benjamin, tall, handsome, moody, jealous and obstinate.

Sheba Son of Bicri, a Benjamite – a troublemaker.

Solomon Son of David and Bathsheba, builder of the temple and successor to David as king over Judah and Israel. A king renowned for his great wealth and wisdom.

Tamar David's beautiful daughter, sister of Absalom, and raped by her half-brother Amnon.

Uriah A Hittite, a senior army officer and one of David's thirty mighty men.

Zadok Joint priest with – and eventual successor to – Abiathar.

Ziba Mephibosheth's steward.

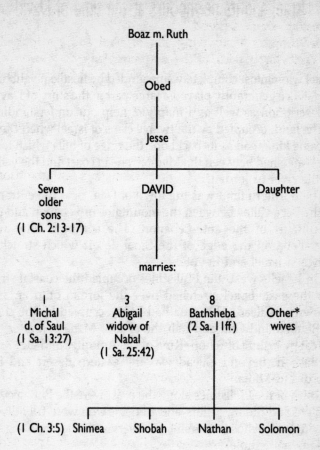

Boaz m. Ruth

Obed

Jesse

| Seven older sons (1 Ch. 2:13-17) | DAVID | Daughter |

marries:

| 1 Michal d. of Saul (1 Sa. 13:27) | 3 Abigail widow of Nabal (1 Sa. 25:42) | 8 Bathsheba (2 Sa. 11ff.) | Other* wives |

(1 Ch. 3:5)   Shimea   Shobah   Nathan   Solomon

* Eight of David's wives are
mentioned by name in the Bible.

Israel and its neighbours at the time of David

Israel was almost completely surrounded by hostile neighbours and, since geography played a large part in the story of David, a description as well as a map will help our understanding.

The land, occupied by the twelve clans of Israel when David became king, had as its backbone the ridge of hills which form the watershed between the Mediterranean coast and the valley of the river of Jordan.

The northern limit was the town of Dan, near the entrance to the Beca valley between the mountains of Lebanon and the mountains of the ante-Lebanon. The southern limit was Beersheba on the edge of the Sinai desert which stretched between Israel and Egypt.

On Israel's west, the Philistines occupied the coastal strip. On the east, Israel stretched over the Jordan onto an area known as Gilead. This area had been occupied by the clans of Reuben and Gad and half the clan of Manasseh after the defeat by Joshua of Sihon, King of the Amorites and Og, King of Bashan. Beyond Gilead was the eastern desert and the 'hordes of Midian'.

North of the Philistines along the coast were the Phoenicians of Tyre and Sidon, sailors and traders, who were friendly to David and whose craftsmen supervised the building of Solomon's temple.

A little inland from Tyre and Sidon was the kingdom of Geshur, whose royal princess bore David a handsome son, Absalom.

East of Geshur was the friendly King of Hamath, also allied to David, in the Beca Valley between the mountains of Lebanon and those of ante-Lebanon, as strategic then as it is now.

To the east of Hamath, and east of the mountains of ante-Lebanon, were the powerful Arameans, who allied themselves to the Ammonites south of Gilead to attack David.

The kingdom of Ammon had remained intact to the south

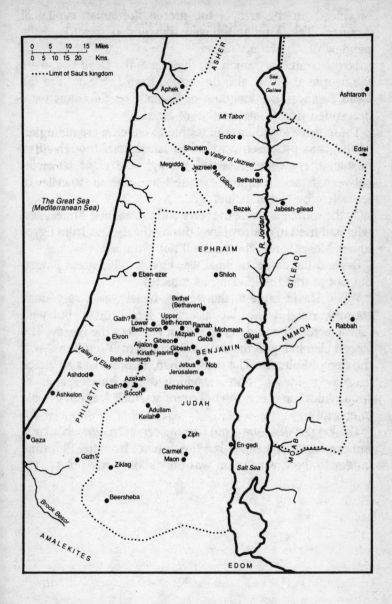

The scale shown reads:

```
0    5    10   15   Miles
0   5  10  15  20   Kms.
······ Limit of Saul's kingdom
```

Map labels:

ASHER

Aphek

Sea of Galilee

Ashtaroth

Mt Tabor

Endor

Shunem   Valley of Jezreel

Megiddo   Jezreel   Mt Gilboa   Bethshan

Edrei

The Great Sea
(Mediterranean Sea)

Bezek   Jabesh-gilead

R. Jordan

EPHRAIM

GILEAD

Eben-ezer   Shiloh

Bethel
(Bethaven)

Upper
Gath?   Beth-horon
Lower   Beth-horon   Ramah
Ekron   Beth-horon   Mizpah   Michmash
Aijalon   Gibeon   Geba   Gilgal
Kiriath-jearim   Gibeah   BENJAMIN
Beth-shemesh   Jebus   Nob
Jerusalem

AMMON

Rabbah

Ashdod

Gath?   Azekah
Ashkelon   Socoh   Bethlehem

JUDAH

PHILISTIA

Adullam
Keilah

Ziph

Gaza

Carmel   En-gedi
Maon

Gath?   Ziklag

Salt Sea

MOAB

Beersheba

Brook Besor

AMALEKITES

EDOM

The founding of the Hebrew monarchy

13

of Gilead, in the area of the present Jordanian capital of Amman. The Ammonites were descended from Lot, the nephew of Abraham.

To the south of Ammon, on the east of the Dead Sea, were the people of Moab, also descended from Lot. South of the Dead Sea was the kingdom of Edom. The Edomites were descended from Esau, brother of Israel.

These three kingdoms, all related to Israel, were not a part of the land promised by God to Israel and, though often hostile, they were preserved through the eight centuries between Israel's original conquest and the destruction of Jerusalem by Nebuchadnezzar.

To the south-east were the fierce and threatening Amalakites, who had tried to destroy Israel during the exodus from Egypt under Moses, and who had still not given up.

Beyond the desert of Sinai was Egypt, still a great power, but not at that time flexing its muscles.

When David came to the throne, Israel was a very small country, roughly the dimensions of Israel today, but with Gilead across the Jordan and without most of the Negev. The largest clan living in the area of the present 'West Bank' was the clan of Ephraim. The danger then, as now, was an attack from two sides at once. David had the interior lines of communication across the hill country which was impassable to chariots.

The longest distance, from Dan to Beersheba, was about one hundred and forty miles, but the distance from the Philistine border to the River Jordan was only about forty miles.

Introduction

David was a military genius, ranking with Alexander the Great, Julius Caesar and Napoleon Bonaparte. From his use of the sling against the clumsily armed Goliath to the surprise attacks by his fleet-footed veterans on whole armies of horsemen and chariots, he was a master of the unexpected. He also knew how to exploit Israel's interior lines of communication against its encircling enemies by swift marches from north to south and back again. David kept his access to the sea through a friendly Tyre and to both the north and to Syria's western flank through a friendly ruler in Hamath – today's Beka Valley.

Like every great commander, his winning streak and his incredible personal bravery inspired a fierce loyalty in his army, especially among the band of veterans who had followed him ever since they were all outlaws together, weaving in and out through the desert fringe of Judah to avoid King Saul and his army.

Not many great commanders, however, have had David's matching political genius. History is littered with military commanders who seized power by force and then, without any popular support, had to hold on to it by force. David was no revolutionary. Despite severe provocation and two easy opportunities to assassinate King Saul, and despite his anointing as Saul's successor by the great judge Samuel who had previously anointed Saul, he did nothing to claim the crown until Saul was killed in a battle against the Philistines.

Even then, David waited until summoned by his own tribe, Judah, to be their king, and he waited again for several years until the other tribes came to Judah to ask him to rule them too. This careful build-up of political support established a lasting respect for the monarchy, and his dynasty lasted until the destruction of Jerusalem by the Babylonians hundreds of years later.

David captured Jerusalem from the Jebusites to establish a

federal capital on neutral ground between the northern tribes and Judah and there, to administer the whole kingdom. He built up Israel's first civil service and established the nation's centre of worship.

Exceptionally for a military genius he was also a great poetic visionary and, though we have lost his original music, his songs have continued to be sung now for nearly three thousand years, a record which is unmatched and probably unmatchable. Seldom has anyone been able to see into the heart of a great man as he faces the major crises of his life as we see, through these songs, into the heart of David. And few men or women, great or humble, have been able to express the very human emotions which find an echo in each of our hearts.

Those who fight the belief that hymns can be sung only to organ music, and those who want to make a case for some physical exuberance in singing, can take great comfort from David. He wanted his songs to be expressed to the full and his list of instruments may cheer the hearts of those who want variety in church music.

Music was part of David's being and we first meet him as a talented young musician playing a harp to charm away the black moods of a depressive king. When he became king, he set up a royal choir. He composed their music as well as their words, taught others to compose too and taught all the people to sing.

David was also an architect of genius. Solomon built the temple, but David designed it. Although the temple has disappeared, there are those who believe that the classical beauty of its design, renowned through the ancient world, was taken up by the Persians and passed on by them to the Greeks, so that in looking today at the style and proportions of the great temple on the Acropolis, we are seeing some remnant of the genius of David.

David was no cold genius, but a man of great human warmth. He gave and received undying friendship and loyalty. His friendship with Jonathan was strong and secure across the great divide of self-interest which separated them, and Jonathan's loyalty to David drove his father to despair of his son's political sense. Much later, David's lament for his rebellious son Absalom drove Joab, the army commander, to similar exasperation. His uninhibited dancing, as the ark of God came into Jerusalem, drove his wife, Michal, to rebuke him for behaviour unfitting for a king. She never forgot that she was a king's daughter. It is in his songs above all, however, that he lays out for us all to see his fears and hopes, his bewilderment and faith, his passion for justice and truth and his horror at his awful lapses from the law of the God he loved. There are few public figures who have been so open and so human.

Both Jews and Christians look back to David as a man of faith in God. When Shakespeare's Macbeth was told by the witches that he would be King of Scotland, he took to murder in order to make sure that the prophecy came true. David did the opposite. Although Samuel had anointed him when he was only a young shepherd, and although God clearly had deserted King Saul, David possessed the faith to wait for God to clear the way to the throne. It was David's faith in the power of God which made him volunteer to take on the Philistine giant, Goliath, in single combat; a faith which gave him the courage to discard the heavy defensive armour and rely on his shepherd's sling. After he became king, faith gave him the courage to launch a surprise attack against the first Philistine invasion without waiting for the mobilization of Israel. Except for one quickly repented lapse, it was faith which made him fight all his wars without the organization of a standing army and without the expensive military hardware of the day. Above all, he had faith in the word of God who had revealed himself to Israel through the patriarchs and then, more fully, through Moses. He had great reverence for the law of God, for its goodness and justice, and believed that there, and there alone, was the true way of life. Like the later prophets he also saw that he would have a descendant greater than himself, a Messiah through whom salvation would come to God's chosen people.

There was a dark side to David's life. He was not allowed to build the temple because, God told him, he was a 'man of blood'. There is no doubt that in establishing Israel's borders against those who wanted to exterminate the nation, he was carrying out God's will. Just as it was inappropriate, however, for any king to officiate in God's holy house, so a king who had shed so much blood was not the appropriate builder of the house of God. Those of us who live in a secure and peaceful country find it harder than those who have lived through war and terror to understand the ferocity with which people will defend themselves against extermination. After a war is won, and in the security of peace, we can ask whether this or that action was necessary to defend ourselves. Even in those rough days, however, the law of Moses condemned the taking of innocent blood and there is no doubt that, by that law, David, though more lenient than the kings of his time, was sometimes guilty.

David had another fatal flaw. Though Abraham and Jacob had taken concubines, and though Jacob had two wives, the people of Israel seem mainly to have followed the monogamous Isaac and Rebekah. Every recorded story of a marriage of more than one wife is a story of trouble, and the books of Moses give the monogamous Adam and Eve as God's original pattern for marriage. David's adultery, and the murder and cover-up which followed, had their roots in his breach of the law of Moses which forbad the king to take many wives.

Although David was anguished and wholehearted in his repentance, the quarrels and fratricide between the children of his various wives continued until David's death. And he left a bad example to his successor. Where David counted his wives on the fingers of both hands, Solomon counted them in hundreds. Those wives perverted his faith and, for generations, the faith of his people.

Yet for all his faults, God recognized David's faith and honoured it. Not only did God preserve the dynasty, but it was to David's line that the great Redeemer was promised. We should not judge David more harshly.

Part I

History

I
David and Goliath

The two armies stood on opposite slopes with a valley between. On the western side were the Philistines, the sea people from the coastal plain, the fierce invaders. On the eastern slope clustered the people of Israel, the hill folk, brought together by their first king to guard their homes, flocks and farms.

At the last encounter Saul, their new king, had routed the Philistines and his son, Jonathan, had been the hero of the day. So the Philistines hesitated to attack. But Israel, too, hesitated to launch a straight frontal assault. They had won their last victory against the much heavier numbers of the Philistines by a brilliant tactical surprise, but they could not rely on carrying that off twice.

The Philistines suggested that the deadlock should be broken by single combat between champions. They felt confident in their extraordinary ten-foot giant with his heavy armour. Israel, however, had no-one to match Goliath. Their king was a head taller than anyone in Israel and Jonathan's courage and daring had won them the last battle, but neither of them could counter the great reach of the giant's sword.

David, youngest son of Jesse of Bethlehem, came about fifteen miles to the army of Israel to bring provisions for his older brothers. When he arrived, after a very early start, he found Goliath coming out, as he had been doing for forty days, to shout defiance and to smile as he watched the terrified Israelites scattering in front of him.

As the young David saw this, he was outraged. It was not so much at the sight of the panic in Israel's army, not even at the insult to Israel of the arrogant giant. Rather, David believed that Israel's God was the God, the almighty Creator of heaven and earth, awesome and all-powerful. He led Israel out of Egyptian slavery, across the dry bed of the Red Sea, and helped them defeat all their enemies, giving them the land of Canaan and helping them, miraculously, to defend it against all comers.

21

Israel's God was not a carved stick or stone, but was alive and active. So David asked indignantly, 'Who is this uncircumcised Philistine that he should defy the armies of the living God?' As for Israel, he continued, could they be terrified when God was on their side?

His brothers recognized his voice and came over. What an embarrassment! A younger brother, who knew nothing of war, coming along with loud-mouthed criticism of all their comrades. Eliab, the eldest, decided to put him in his place.

'Why have you come down here? And with whom did you leave those few sheep in the desert? I know how conceited you are and how wicked your heart is; you came down only to watch the battle.'

David answered just like any younger brother: 'What have I done? Can't I even speak?'

Samuel's anointing of David

But David was not just any younger brother. Some time earlier Samuel, the judge, who had ruled Israel before King Saul, visited David's father Jesse and his family at their home in Bethlehem. God had told Samuel that, because of the king's disobedience, he had rejected Saul as ruler over his people Israel and that Samuel should go to Bethlehem to anoint one of the sons of Jesse as king.

Saul's way with dissidents was well known and Samuel was alarmed. He objected that, if Saul found out about this, he would kill him. God was understanding and replied that he should go to Bethlehem to offer a sacrifice which would be seen as part of his normal duties and so cover his dangerous mission. So when Samuel arrived, he suggested to Jesse and his family that he should prepare them for the sacrifice.

As Samuel, in the ordinary course of introductions, met in turn Jesse's six sons who were at home, God told him that each was not the son of his choice. Finally a puzzled Samuel asked Jesse whether there were any more sons. Jesse said, 'There is still the youngest, but he is tending the sheep.'

Since Samuel refused to sit down until young David arrived, they sent for him. He was not as outstanding to look at as Eliab the eldest, but he had a fresh and open face. This time God told Samuel that he was the one, so Samuel anointed him in front of his family.

It was clear from Eliab's brusque answer to David on the battlefield, however, that he and the other brothers had not yet any clear idea of why Samuel had anointed David. But there was an immediate change in David himself and we read, 'From that day on the Spirit of the Lord came upon David in power.'

David's consciousness of God, of his holiness, power and concern for his people, was suddenly sharpened. So David did not see Goliath merely as the powerful giant whose reach was longer and whose armour was stronger than those of anyone in Israel. He saw him as someone who deserved divine judgment for daring to defy the living God. Not at all discouraged by his older brother, David would not be put down. He kept on asking what was to be done – until at last the king himself heard of it and sent for him.

David's tactics

David came straight to the point. He said that no-one should lose heart on account of this Philistine and that he would go out and fight him. Saul naturally objected that David was only a boy and that Goliath had been a fighting man from his youth. But David rejoined that he had killed both a lion and a bear which had at different times come after his sheep. He than added the point which really made him confident despite his youth and inexperience: 'This uncircumcised Philistine will be like one of them because he has defied the armies of the living God. The LORD who delivered me from the paw of the lion and the paw of the bear will deliver me from the hand of this Philistine.'

Saul finally agreed to the venture and put his own armour on David. But when David tried to walk round in it he found it clumsy, said that he wasn't used to it and insisted on taking it all off again. He chose instead to fight with the weapon he was familiar with, preferring to attack the heavily armoured, slow moving Goliath by a lightning strike with a stone from his shepherd's sling. This would enable him to hit the giant while still well out of his reach.

His tactic might well need more than one shot and so he needed space to retreat and try again. We read that 'as the Philistine moved closer to attack him, David ran quickly towards the battle line to meet him'. On the way he took five smooth stones for his shepherd's sling from a stream running along the valley floor. Once over the stream and on the Philistine slope, he closed as fast as he could to get the best aim at the vulnerable part of Goliath's head, the small part outside the protection of his helmet. If he missed with the first stone, he had now put enough space behind him and had enough speed to keep out of range of the sword and spear, so he could take aim several times.

Goliath looked at this fresh-faced youth approaching with only a staff and sling and was outraged: 'Am I a dog, that you come at me with sticks?'

David told him – and the listening armies – 'You come against me with sword and spear and javelin, but I come against you in the name of the LORD God Almighty, the God of the armies of Israel whom you have defied . . . Today I will give the carcasses of the Philistine army to the birds of the air and the beasts of the earth, and the whole world will know that there is a God in Israel. All those gathered here will know that it is not by sword or spear that the LORD saves; for the battle is the LORD's, and he will give all of you into our hands.'

The first stone found its target and the giant fell face down on the ground. David ran forward, took Goliath's own sword and cut off his head to make quite certain that both armies knew that the unbelievable had happened and that the Philistine champion would never rise again.

The effect on the armies was electric. The Philistines turned and ran. The men of Israel chased them all the way to Goliath's home town of Gath, several miles away, and the other capital city of Ekron, much further away, and the Philistine dead were strewn along the roads.

The outcome was a great victory for Israel, but the hero of the day was David, this young shepherd who had volunteered as Israel's champion when no-one else, from the king down, would take on the role. In front of the whole army he had killed, single-handed, a giant in full armour.

This was not only an immensely brave and daring act, it also showed the tactical genius for which David was to become famous. The ten-foot giant could not be killed with the conventional weapons because Goliath's sword and spear could outreach everyone else. There were no volunteers because everyone thought in conventional terms and no-one could see a way around the problem. But David, the shepherd, knew that the sling-shot could be a deadly weapon in skilled hands. In the time shortly before Samuel became judge, we read of seven hundred soldiers from the tribe of Benjamin 'each of whom could sling a stone at a hair and not miss' (Judges 20:16). David had gained this skill while using the sling in defending his sheep against the wild animals which threatened them.

David's faith

All the same, use of this weapon against a heavily armoured soldier needed not only skill, but great self-confidence, nerves of steel and a bravery which did not come from lack of imagination – of which David had plenty – or from foolish self-confidence, but from the highest possible motivation, his faith in God. That faith sustained him while his own life was at stake as well as the lives of the army behind him, an army which could have panicked just as quickly as the Philistines, had the duel gone the wrong way.

We see in this first fight the motive which guided David throughout his life. It was not his own reputation or even that of Israel which moved him. He was driven by his outrage on hearing the sneers of Goliath against the people of the living God. The Philistines needed to be shown that the God whom Israel worshipped was the true God. He was alive to hear the sneers and to defend his honour. David's extraordinary bravery was sustained by the belief that if he gave of his best, God would honour him and protect him. His reply to Goliath showed that he put his confidence in God rather than in his own skill.

David and Saul

When David came back from the valley, still holding Goliath's head, Saul asked him whose son he was. David told him, 'I am the son of your servant Jesse of Bethlehem.'

Rulers like to be able to pin down those who have, in one way or another, gained some power in public affairs. David, who fought with the highest motives, did not know yet the political power which came with public acclamation. But Saul knew. Footloose heroes can be dangerous. They needed to be reminded that, in a patriarchal society where a son has to take note of his father's wishes, a father can be held responsible for his son's behaviour and that family properties are vulnerable to royal power. A ruler reaches naturally for the levers of counter-pressure which can be used to keep over-mighty subjects in line.

It is probable that Saul knew perfectly well who David was, for another of his skills had already brought David to court. He had such a reputation as a skilled musician that when the king became subject to fits of acute depression, the courtiers sent for David to see whether his music could bring the king back to a better frame of mind. Saul cannot have been an easy audience. Samuel had already told him that God had rejected him as king and, since that time, only David's music had been able to lift him out of the fits of depression. It must have been enchanting music, brilliantly and sensitively played. But a musician is not such a power in the land as a popular hero and Saul had no need then to mention David's father; it was enough that David's music relieved and calmed his nerves.

David: poet and musician

Yet his music and poetry were almost as important to David throughout his life as his soldiering. Indeed when his days of battle were over, he returned to his first love, the songs and music which he had begun to compose as a shepherd on the Judean hills. We have a flavour of this early period in his best-known song, still sung all over the world three thousand years later.

The LORD is my shepherd, I shall
   lack nothing.
  He makes me lie down in green
   pastures,
he leads me beside quiet waters,
  he restores my soul.
He guides me in the paths of
   righteousness
  for his name's sake.
Even though I walk
  through the valley of the shadow
   of death,
I will fear no evil,
  for you are with me;
your rod and your staff,
  they comfort me.

You prepare a table before me
  in the presence of my enemies.
You anoint my head with oil;
  my cup overflows.
Surely goodness and love will
   follow me
  all the days of my life,
and I will dwell in the house of the
   LORD
  for ever.

                    (Psalm 23)

There may be those who feel that this psalm is too
sentimental for our rough world today. Our own popular music
often reflects a mood of complaint and despair. But when we
think of the background against which David wrote that psalm,
the contrast is not between his times and ours, but between
his faith in God and the lack of faith in our own generation.

It was in that spirit of total trust in a God who was alive and
who loved and protected those who put their trust in him that
the young David had gone out to fight Goliath.

David's ancestry

David also came from a family with a long record of faith in their God. His father Jesse was a man of faith as shown by his readiness to receive Samuel and to present all his sons when the prophet asked to prepare them for the sacrifice in Bethlehem. Jesse's grandmother was Ruth, a Moabitess. David would have known that she gave up the gods of her own country, when she and her Israelite mother-in-law, Naomi, were both widowed. She insisted on going back from Moab with Naomi to Bethlehem, telling her, 'Your people will be my people and your God my God.'

Ruth married Boaz, who was descended from Rahab, a Canaanite woman who had been a prostitute in pagan Jericho; but because she came to believe in the God of Israel, she helped two Israelite spies to escape from Jericho. Her faith saved her and her family when Jericho was taken and she later married an Israelite (the romantic may like to believe it was one of the spies whose lives she saved), and settled down among the people of God.

Saul's jealousy

Newly arrived in Saul's entourage as a soldier, David made fast friends with Jonathan, the king's son, who shared both his faith in God and the same daring spirit in battle. They were kindred souls between whom was absolutely no jealousy and they stuck to each other through pressures which would shatter any normal friendship. Their mutual trust was unbreakable and their mutual love and respect wholehearted.

Jonathan's respect for David showed itself first in the small things. David could not come to court dressed like that! David had nothing but his simple shepherd's clothes, so Jonathan fitted him with his own tunic, sword, bow and belt, to match the clothes of the other officers. Once David was at court, Saul would not let him return home, but gave him a high rank in the army and that pleased the people and the other soldiers too. Soon, however, David became much too popular for Saul's liking. When the army returned home, the people came out

28

singing and dancing; but the refrain of their song was, 'Saul has slain his thousands, and David his tens of thousands.'

That set fire to Saul's worst fears and he muttered, 'What can he get but the kingdom.'

David's misfortune was that Saul, the first king of Israel, was in no mood to tolerate rivalry. Under the tuition of Samuel the king had started well. Saul knew that since Israel had escaped from Egypt and become a nation, God had protected those leaders who had trusted in him. He had brought them out of Egypt despite the overwhelming power of Pharaoh's army, and had protected them in the desert from the fierce Amalakites, who had attacked them without provocation. The Lord had helped them to overcome the kings of Midian on the eastern borders of Canaan and, under Joshua, had enabled them to overcome the much greater numbers against them in Canaan. In spite of the fact that they were often unfaithful to him, God had sent them a succession of faithful judges who had protected them against repeated attacks by greatly superior forces.

Through Samuel, the last of the great judges of Israel, God made Saul king. Saul was brave, simple, modest and religious, but, despite Samuel's instruction, he did not respect the limits of his position as God's vice-regent for his special people, Israel. It was Israel's duty to keep burning the knowledge of the one true God in the darkness of idolatry. So that they could do that, God gave them Canaan and kept them safe from their enemies. Despite Samuel's teaching that faith in God mattered more than military power, however, Saul did not have the faith to trust in God's power. He did not wait for Samuel to carry out the sacrifices before setting out for battle, because, as he waited, he saw his men melting away and he was afraid. Samuel arrived just as Saul had finished the sacrifices. He rebuked him for not keeping God's command and told him that his kingdom would not endure.

'You acted foolishly,' Samuel scolded. 'You have not kept the command the LORD your God gave you; if you had, he would have established your kingdom over Israel for all time. But now your kingdom will not endure; the LORD has sought out a man after his own heart and appointed him leader over his people, because you have not kept the LORD's command.'

Despite that terrible prophecy, Saul's remaining six hundred men defeated the Philistines because of the initiative and leadership of his son, Jonathan. Tragically, however, Saul did not learn from that experience. Later God told him, through Samuel, that he should totally destroy the Amalakites and all their livestock. But, after the battle, Saul took some Amalakite livestock as plunder and kept their king, Agag, alive.

Both this and his previous disobedience were public acts of rebellion by the leader who was meant to set Israel an example. Both these showed a complete lack of faith in God and an absence of respect for his law. Twice was enough and this time a grieving Samuel told him, 'The LORD has torn the kingdom of Israel from you today and has given it to one of your neighbours – to one better than you. He who is the Glory of Israel does not lie or change his mind; for he is not a man, that he should change his mind.'

From that day on Samuel had never seen Saul again.

Instead, unknown to Saul, God had sent Samuel to Jesse of Bethlehem, telling him, 'I have chosen one of his sons to be king.' So, although Saul did not know that Samuel had anointed David in a family ceremony, he could not forget Samuel's prophecy and was on the lookout for rivals. When he heard David praised more than the king, Saul – morose, touchy and resentful – eyed David. He knew that God was no longer with him, but could see from David's success that he was certainly with the young warrior. His fits of frenzy returned. Although David was now a senior army commander, he was as content to play the harp to calm him as he had been while he was only a shepherd. An evil and destructive mood took hold of Saul and, while David was playing, he hurled a spear at him, intending to pin him to the wall. The king missed and threw again, but both times David's lightning response saved him. Saul, though, had not totally lost control. There was a low cunning in his actions. To cover himself he had gone through the motions of 'prophesying' so that it looked as if he was acting in a divinely inspired trance as part of the prophecy. It probably fooled no-one, but enabled the court members to pretend to him and to each other that the near miss was accidental.

With David's escape from death, Saul was now really afraid that God not only had left him, but was with David, so he sent him off to the front line as a commander of a thousand soldiers, hoping that the Philistines would succeed where he had failed.

Far from falling to the Philistines, David was successful in all his campaigns. This greatly reinforced Saul's fear that God himself was protecting David.

Saul plots against David

At this point a wiser king might have wondered whether, if God was with David, he could really succeed in disposing of him. But Saul's mood was not logical. He seems from now on to be trying desperately to kill David, if only to prove that God was not with him. He now promised his elder daughter, Merab, to David if he fought bravely against the Philistines, thinking 'I will not raise a hand against him, let the Philistines do that.' He should, by right, have given David Merab earlier for his victory against Goliath. David replied that he was not worthy to be the king's son-in-law and Saul married her to someone else.

The idea of using a marriage against David stayed with Saul and, when he heard that his second daughter Michal had fallen in love with the young soldier, he offered her to him in return for a hundred Philistine foreskins. David could survive border patrols, but if he had to lead such a raid, he might never come back.

This was a real challenge and one which David the soldier promptly accepted. He soon came back accounting not just for a hundred but for two hundred of Israel's enemies. We don't have to imagine David's thoughts about Saul. He speaks (Psalm 55) of one whose words 'were smooth as butter, but murder was in his heart'. Yet he showed extraordinary restraint. He did not complain nor, as a popular figure might well have done, did he raise a party against the king. He behaved wisely in protesting that he was not worthy to be the

31

king's son-in-law and in counting it an honour to accept the king's challenge. Though after he had married Michal he could have claimed some months with his wife before going to war again, he went straight on with his military service without complaining.

All Saul's efforts to put him in danger only consolidated his hold on the affection of the people. Saul, therefore, gave outright orders to Jonathan and his servants to kill David, putting their loyalty to him in direct conflict with their strong affection for David. So obsessed was he, that he did not even bother to produce false accusations of treachery; he did not even have the cover of the two witnesses which were needed before anyone could be found guilty under Israel's law.

Saul's folly was extraordinary. Before David arrived on the scene he had already tested both the loyalty of the army and of Jonathan by making a foolish oath to execute anyone found eating before night put an end to the pursuit of the Philistines. Jonathan had routed them almost single-handed after all but six hundred of Saul's army had melted away and had then, without knowing of Saul's oath, eaten some wild honey during the pursuit. Saul, for the sake of the oath, prepared to execute him. But the army absolutely refused to go along with such folly and rescued Jonathan. Now Saul was again prepared to risk the loyalty of both Jonathan and the army for his insistence on David's death. Jonathan at once warned David that his father was looking for a chance to kill him and told him to go into hiding. Meantime he spoke well of David to his father: 'Let not the king do wrong to his servant David; he has not wronged you, and what he has done has benefited you greatly. He took his life in his hands when he killed the Philistine. The LORD won a great victory for Israel, and you saw it and were glad. Why then would you do wrong to an innocent man like David by killing him for no reason?'

Saul accepted Jonathan's point and took an oath that he would not kill David. Jonathan then told David and brought him back to court.

Once more the Philistines attacked and once more David won a great victory, but Saul's jealousy again got the better of him and while David was playing the harp, Saul again tried to pin him to the wall with his spear. David swiftly avoided the spear and escaped.

David flees for his life

This time there was no going back. Now that David had a wife and home, Saul thought he had him trapped, so he gave orders for the house to be watched, declaring that, in the morning, David was to be killed. He had reckoned, however, without Michal's devotion to her husband. She let him down through a window and he got safely away.

David has given us his thoughts in Psalm 59:

> Deliver me from evildoers
> and save me from bloodthirsty men.
>
> See how they lie in wait for me!
> Fierce men conspire against me
> for no offence or sin of mine,
> O LORD.
>
> They return at evening,
> snarling like dogs
> and prowl about the city.
> O my Strength, I watch for you;
> you, O God, are my fortress,
> my loving God.

In the morning the king's servants demanded that David be brought before Saul. Michal, playing for time to give David a good start, said that he was ill and put a dummy in the bed. So that he himself could kill David, Saul demanded that the sick man be brought in his bed, but when they came to fetch him, they discovered Michal's trick. She had given him the time he needed. By then he was out of immediate danger.

David instinctively ran to Samuel who was at Naioth, where he presided over the school of the prophets. Samuel, as a prophet of God, had promised him the throne and was the natural person to advise him.

Saul soon found out David's whereabouts and sent soldiers to capture him. As soon as they came within sight of Samuel and his prophets, Saul's men started to prophesy too and forgot their mission. After this had happened to three groups of his men, Saul decided to go himself, but on the road to Naioth the spirit of prophecy came on Saul also. When he got there he stripped off his robes and lay without them all that day and night.

This odd incident shows that God can strike awe into the worst of men and make them acknowledge him. Saul's was only a temporary insight, however, and it passed away, leaving the king's evil intentions unchanged.

David and Jonathan

While Saul was gripped by the prophetic vision at Naioth, David slipped back to see Jonathan, the only friend who could help him. The king's son tried to reassure his friend, saying that his father did nothing without consulting him. David's reaction was that the king, because he knew Jonathan's affection for David, clearly had not told him his intention, and he sombrely concluded that 'there is only a step between me and death'.

David reminded Jonathan of their covenant before the Lord and said that, if he had breached it, then Jonathan should kill him himself. Jonathan unhesitatingly reconfirmed his promise and appealed to God as witness. He made David promise that, if they had to part and if God was with David, then he would never cut off his kindness to Jonathan's family. They made another covenant together and David reaffirmed his oath of love for Jonathan. So they arranged that when, at the New Moon Festival the next day, David's place at the king's table was empty, Jonathan would tell his father that he had given David permission to go home for the annual sacrifice for the whole clan. (At such a sacrifice the whole family should be present, including David.) Jonathan believed that the affair would blow over. David, however, was not convinced. If Saul

34

did not accept the excuse, and wanted David there when he should have been with his own family, it could only be because he intended to do him harm. Whether or not the king accepted this reason for David's absence, Jonathan would go to a rendezvous, taking a boy to carry his bow and arrows. If it was safe for David to return, Jonathan would shoot an arrow and then call to the boy that the arrows were to the side of him. If it was not safe, he would call that the arrows were beyond him. David himself was sure what the answer would be, but he must have wanted Jonathan to see it for himself.

On the first day, Saul ignored David's absence, but on the second he asked Jonathan why David was not there and Jonathan gave his excuse. Saul flared up at once, calling Jonathan a bastard, a traitor and a fool – because so long as David was alive Jonathan would never be king. He ordered Jonathan, 'Now send and bring him to me that he may die.' Jonathan asked what David had done to deserve that and Saul's reply was to hurl his spear at him to kill him. That settled the question beyond dispute.

Next morning Jonathan went out to the rendezvous, shot his arrow and shouted to the boy that the arrow was beyond him. But he could not let David go without seeing him again, so he sent the boy home with the weapons and David came out of hiding. It was an emotional and bitter parting. Jonathan, refusing his father's command, sent David away in peace with the Lord as witness to their covenant between their descendants. They met again only once, in secret in a wood, while Saul was still hunting David.

The friendship between Jonathan and David is one of the great friendships of history. Both were young soldiers, both showed exceptional bravery and leadership. Both were in line for the leadership of their country. But there was no jealousy or envy. Both admired each other's qualities. They were prepared to trust each other and to risk their lives for each other. Long afterwards, David did not forget the promise he had made to protect Jonathan's family.

David's short and distinguished career as a serving officer was over. He was now an outlaw.

The outcasting of David marked the moment the rule of law in Israel – so carefully set out by Moses – was displaced by arbitrary tyranny. The soldier who had saved Israel from the Philistines, the hero of both army and people, was running for his life. Instead of enforcing the law, the king was breaking it and his obsession was being backed by the sword. It was a terrible time for David and a terrible time for all in Israel who trusted in God and believed in his law. Worse was to come.

2
Outlaw

It was at last clear to David that his position as a leader in the king's army was at an end, that Saul really wanted his life and that Jonathan, the king's own son, could not protect him.

Nor could Samuel protect him. Instead David made his way to Nob, near Jebus (what was to be Jerusalem), to Ahimelech the priest. Ahimelech was terrified to find him almost alone and evidently a fugitive. But he 'enquired of the LORD for him' and also, when pressed, gave him bread and the only weapon the priest had: Goliath's sword. David said that there was no sword like it and took it.

David, perhaps to protect Ahimelech as well as himself, did not admit that he was an outlaw. He told Ahimelech that he was on a secret mission for the king and was on his way to meet his men. But it did not save Ahimelech from Saul. Doeg, the Edomite, who had an important post as master of Saul's herds, was also there, and saw what was going on.

When Doeg returned to Saul he found him holding court under a tamarisk tree and accusing his officials of being in conspiracy with David and Jonathan against him. Doeg reported how he had seen Ahimelech give David Goliath's sword. He did not say that David had told Ahimelech that he was on a mission for Saul – which might have exonerated the high priest. Saul sent at once for Ahimelech and all his priestly family and accused him of being in the conspiracy.

With great dignity, Ahimelech responded: 'Who of all your servants is as loyal as David, the king's son-in-law, captain of your bodyguard and highly respected in your household? Was that day the first time I enquired of God for him? Of course not! Let not the king accuse your servant or any of his father's family, for your servant knows nothing at all about this whole affair.'

The murder of Ahimelech, and David's faith

Without trial, without saying why he did not accept

37

Ahimelech's plea, without the two witnesses required by the law, Saul alone, in his paranoia and the heat of passion, ordered his guards to turn and kill Ahimelech and, though they had not even been accused, all his family too. The guards and officials were men of Israel, however, and bravely refused. So then Saul turned to Doeg, who was an Edomite without such scruples, and the accuser. Doeg not only killed the eighty-five priests who were there, but 'he also put to the sword Nob, the town of the priests with its men and women, its children and infants, and its cattle, donkeys and sheep'. Only Ahimelech's son Abiathar escaped to join David. The depths of David's reaction to Doeg's treachery are given in Psalm 52:

> Why do you boast of evil, you mighty man?
>> Why do you boast all day long,
>> you who are a disgrace in the
>>> eyes of God?
> Your tongue plots destruction;
>> it is like a sharpened razor,
>> you who practise deceit.
> You love evil rather than good,
>> falsehood rather than speaking
>>> the truth.
> You love every harmful word,
>> O you deceitful tongue!

> Surely God will bring you down to
>> everlasting ruin;
> He will snatch you up and tear
>> you from your tent;
> he will uproot you from the land
>> of the living.
> The righteous will see and fear;
>> they will laugh at him saying,
> 'Here now is the man
>> who did not make God his stronghold
> but trusted in his great wealth
>> and grew strong by destroying others!'

> But I am like an olive tree
>   flourishing in the house of God;
> I trust in God's unfailing love
>   for ever and ever.
> I will praise you for ever for what
>   you have done;
>   in your name I will hope, for
>   your name is good.
>   I will praise you in the presence
>   of your saints.

Those are the words of a man whose faith has not been shattered by monstrous and cruel injustice, who still believes that a just God will punish evil, and still wants to praise his God's unfailing love.

By contrast, Saul did not trust in God and suffered from the obsessive suspicions common to rulers, especially to despotic rulers, who have every reason to fear those who have suffered from their despotism. But suspicion does not only grip despots. President Nixon, though democratically elected, and while still having the support of a majority of the American public, was shown to be living in a constant state of paranoia by the tapes of his conversations which were produced in evidence in the Watergate scandal.

Prime ministers, too, when they have been in office long enough to make enemies but not so long as to want to give up, are often said to be 'in the bunker', trusting no-one but their close cronies and deeply suspicious of everyone else. Outside the democracies such a mood can be dangerous. Idi Amin of Uganda was the most spectacular despot of recent years, though Saddam Hussein is said to be even worse, by those who know his actions. By contrast, the person of faith must sit lightly to power, waiting until God gives it and then prepared to give it up when the time has clearly come.

David in Philistia and the borders

At first David headed west across the border to the Philistine territory, where Achish, King of Gath (Goliath's city) gave him

sanctuary. Achish seems to have taken the kind of liking to
David which the great take to a worthy opponent. The king's
servants, however, were suspicious. Seeing this, David
pretended that he had been driven mad by the shock of
disgrace and exile and Achish accepted the pretence and told
his people to send David away. Setting out for the no-man's
land on the border of the desert, David's faith was unshaken,
as Psalm 34 shows:

> I will extol the LORD at all times;
>> his praise will always be on my lips.
> My soul will boast in the LORD;
>> let the afflicted hear and rejoice.
> Glorify the LORD with me;
>> let us exalt his name together.

> I sought the LORD, and he answered me;
>> he delivered me from all my fears.

> Those who look to him are radiant;
>> their faces are never covered with shame.

> This poor man called, and the LORD
>> heard him;
> he saved him out of all his troubles.

> The angel of the LORD encamps
>> around those who fear him,
> and he delivers them.

> Taste and see that the LORD is good;
>> blessed is the man who takes
>> refuge in him.

> Fear the LORD, you his saints,
>> for those who fear him lack nothing.

> The lions may grow weak and hungry,

but those who seek the LORD lack
  no good thing.

Come, my children, listen to me;
  I will teach you the fear of the LORD.
Whoever of you loves life
  and desires to see many good days,
keep your tongue from evil
  and your lips from speaking lies.
Turn from evil and do good;
  seek peace and pursue it.

The eyes of the LORD are on the righteous
  and his ears are attentive to their cry;
the face of the LORD is against those who do evil,
  to cut off the memory of them
    from the earth.

The righteous cry out, and the
    LORD hears them;
  he delivers them from all their troubles.
The LORD is close to the brokenhearted
  and saves those who are crushed
    in spirit.

A righteous man may have many troubles,
  but the LORD delivers him from them all;
he protects all his bones,
  not one of them will be broken.

Evil will slay the wicked;
  the foes of the righteous will be
    condemned.
The LORD redeems his servants;
  no-one who takes refuge in him
    will be condemned.

Those are the words of someone with complete faith in God.

David establishes a base

Leaving Gath hurriedly, David returned east, round the southern border between Judah and the desert, until he neared his own home town south of Bethlehem where there were caves in the hills. In one of these, the cave of Adullam, he set up camp. There his family, now rightly anxious for their own safety, came to join him. Once it began to be known that David was on the borders of Judah, four hundred others also joined, who were in distress or in debt or discontented, and he became their leader.

We have David's prayer for God's help from the cave in Psalm 57:

> Have mercy on me, O God, have
> mercy on me,
> for in you my soul takes refuge.
> I will take refuge in the shadow of
> your wings
> until the disaster has passed.
>
> I cry out to God Most High,
> to God, who fulfils [his purpose] for me.
> He sends from heaven and saves me,
> rebuking those who hotly pursue me;
> God sends his love and his
> faithfulness.
>
> I am in the midst of lions;
> I lie among ravenous beasts –
> men whose teeth are spears and arrows,
> whose tongues are sharp swords.
>
> Be exalted, O God, above the heavens;
> let your glory be over all the earth.
>
> They spread a net for my feet –
> I was bowed down in distress.

> They dug a pit in my path –
>   but they have fallen into it
>   themselves.
>
> My heart is steadfast, O God,
>   my heart is steadfast;
>   I will sing and make music.
> Awake, my soul!
>   Awake, harp and lyre!
>   I will awaken at the dawn.
>
> I will praise you, O Lord, among the
>   nations;
>   I will sing of you among the peoples.
> For great is your love, reaching to
>   the heavens;
>   your faithfulness reaches to the skies.
>
> Be exalted, O God, above the heavens;
>   let your glory be over all the earth.

Support for David grows

This move to the caves was the hinge of David's life, the point at which he became a leader in his own right. From then on he built up his own following until he became king, first of Judah and then of all Israel. Among the family who came to him were Joab, Asahel and Abishai, sons of his sister Zeruiah, who were to be his military commanders. Under Abishai's command were the three most trusty fighters of the band.

The prophet Gad was now there to pray for David, to instruct him and to inquire of God on his behalf. Gad told him to leave the stronghold and go into Judah, so they moved to the forest of Hereth. At this time much of the hill country was rich with woodland. Prior to this David had been to Moab, where his great-grandmother Ruth had come from, and had asked the king to look after his father and mother.

In the forest of Hereth, in the hill country of Judah, David was able publicly to enlist men in his service. Saul had forced him to take up arms, but against Saul and his army he acted only defensively. He was not a guerilla leader set on the overthrow of the government. But there was no such protection to Judah's enemies who came raiding across their desert border. Very soon David heard that the Philistines were robbing the threshing-floors in Keilah, which was in Judah. David asked God, through Gad, whether he should go to the protection of Keilah and he was told to save them. His small band were not so sure that they could take on the Philistines, so David asked again and the answer was the same.

Their first major attack was successful, the Philistines were routed and Keilah relieved. David and his men took the Philistine cattle, the first they could call their own, giving them a degree of self-sufficiency.

Abiathar, the only priest who had escaped Saul's massacre, joined David at Keilah, bringing the ephod, the high priest's sacred tunic, with the Urim and Thummim, two precious stones, sewn on to it. At critical times, when Israel's leaders needed a straight 'yes' or 'no' from the high priest, God would answer (in a way which has not been explained to us) through the Urim and Thummim. Now David, with his tiny band, had both prophet and priest. Saul, with his great army, had neither. An embryonic church and state came into being at Keilah.

Saul pursues David

David had now come out into the open and Saul heard that he had relieved Keilah. Instead of being grateful that David had rescued the town which he should have protected himself, he mounted an expedition for Keilah believing that David was now 'imprisoned by entering a town with gates and bars'. He added, piously, 'God has handed him over to me', making David the dangerous rebel and he the threatened king.

David needed to know whether, under pressure from Saul's forces, the fear of the people of Keilah would outweigh their gratitude. God through Abiathar warned him that the people of Keilah would deliver him to Saul.

In Psalm 35 David says:

> They repay me evil for good
> and leave my soul forlorn.

He did not want another massacre like the one at Nob and, with a band now numbering six hundred after their first success, David left Keilah for the Desert of Ziph, near Hebron. Saul, with his picked bodyguard followed. David could have taken Saul on in the open field. He knew the country and Saul and his guards did not. But, even under this constant pressure, keeping out of Saul's way as he went through the woods and mountains, he did not want to risk the life of God's anointed king. So he slipped and twisted, but never gave fight – and God protected him.

In one of the woods, Jonathan arranged a meeting with David – a meeting which was to be their last. He used it to encourage David, who certainly needed encouraging. He told him that both he and his father knew that David would be the next king and he promised that he would serve David as faithfully as he had served his own father. Finally they made another covenant. Jonathan and David were never to see each other again.

The Ziphites went to Saul at Gibeah to reveal his hideout. They told the king that David was 'in the strongholds of Horesh, on the hill of Hakilah'. They promised that if the king came down, they would hand David over. Saul said piously, 'The Lord bless you' and they went out ahead as Saul's scouts. Saul closed on David in the Desert of Maon in the Arabah, but as they were on opposite sides of the same mountain, Saul was summoned to repel Philistine raids, which were probably – such was the speed of his response – against his own Benjamite territory. David went up into the strongholds of En Gedi, 'The rocks of the wild goats', west of the Dead Sea.

David tells us his feelings in Psalm 54:

45

Save me, O God, by your name;
  vindicate me by your might.
Hear my prayer, O God;
  listen to the words of my mouth.

Strangers are attacking me;
  ruthless men seek my life –
  men without regard for God.

Surely God is my help;
  the Lord is the one who sustains me.

Let evil recoil on those who slander me;
  in your faithfulness destroy them.

I will sacrifice a freewill offering to you;
  I will praise your name, O LORD,
  for it is good.
For he has delivered me from all
  my troubles,
  and my eyes have looked in
  triumph on my foes.

David spares Saul's life

After dealing with the Philistine raids, Saul was back on
David's trail again, this time with three thousand men against
David's faithful six hundred. A ruthless king with troops at
his back easily found servile informants who told him that
David was in En Gedi. Saul's force went to En Gedi and in
one of the caves there, which had probably been enlarged to
provide midday shelter for flocks of sheep, Saul took his siesta.
In the back and sides of the very same cave were David and
his men. As they crouched quietly in the dark, David's men
urged him to kill Saul there and then. They said that God had
clearly delivered him up to David. It could not be a coincidence
that he had come alone to that cave. But David refused.
Circumstances did not alter principles and he would not kill

'the Lord's anointed', but he did cut off a corner of Saul's cloak to show what he could have done, though he later repented even of that minor affront to the king's dignity.

When Saul left the cave, David called after him. He bowed to the ground, showing his respect, and called him 'father'. He reminded him of their family relationship (through his marriage to Michal) and, to avoid confrontation, he blamed evil advisers instead of Saul himself. Then he pointed out the cut in Saul's cloak and asked him why he was afraid of someone who, when it was in his power, had done him no harm. He said that God would judge between them and promised, 'My hand will not touch you.' Finally he appealed to Saul's regal standing by telling him that the chase was beneath the dignity of the King of Israel. Saul was apparently overcome with remorse. In a moment of truth he told David, 'The kingdom of Israel will be established in your hands' and asked him not to cut off his descendants. David gave his oath and Saul returned home to his court at Gibeah. But David knew Saul well enough not to trust his promises and he and his men returned to their rocky stronghold.

It is small wonder that David's men had urged him to kill this jealous, unbalanced, ruthless and bloody king. Worldly wisdom would consider him a fool to lose the chance. It shows something of David's command of his followers that he was able to restrain them. His confrontation of Saul, whose men must have been within call, was an act of outstanding boldness and bravery. But, as his poetry shows, David was not guided by worldly wisdom. He believed firmly that God would judge between Saul and himself, and that meantime God would protect him. Though believing that, however, it took faith of the highest order to confront a king who would not even listen to his own high priest pleading for his life.

David was wise not to trust Saul's tears of remorse. The king had not admitted his fault, only that David was more righteous than he was. Nor had he given David any promises. He prayed that God would be kind to David, but he offered nothing himself. So when Samuel died and that last small moral restraint on Saul was gone, David and his men moved out of

Judah to the Desert of Maon, in the region of Ziph and Carmel.

David and Abigail

In the desert there were no towns like Keilah to attract major raids from Philistines or Amalakites, but sheep farmers with large flocks still needed protection from thieves and minor raids in those sparsely populated border areas. David and his men found themselves in the neighbourhood of a big sheep-farmer called Nabal, and they gave protection to his shepherds against thieves and raiders from the deserts beyond. David and his men were now some distance from those who must have helped to supply them in Judah and they may have had difficulty, while avoiding Saul, in keeping all the livestock they gained at Keilah. So, when shearing time came, with its traditional liberality, David sent some of his young men with a polite message, telling of the protection they had given and asking Nabal to give 'whatever you can find for them'.

Nabal gave him a sour and abusive answer. David's fame had gone the length and breadth of Israel, but he said, 'Who is this David?' and asked why he should give the bread and meat for his shearers to 'men coming from who knows where'.

David's men turned back without reply and when David heard what they had to say, he was incensed. He ordered them to put on their swords and a full four hundred set out with him to show Nabal who David was. Even though he had been sorely provoked, this hasty action was out of character. The iron self-control with which he had confronted Saul gave way to a mood of angry revenge against Nabal. He had told Saul that he was the Lord's anointed and that it was beneath him to go chasing David. David, however, was also the Lord's anointed and it was certainly beneath him to seek revenge on a surly sheep-farmer. David, who left the judgment between himself and Saul to God, now wanted to be judge and executioner of Nabal.

A divine providence prevented him. Nabal had a wife, Abigail, who was as wise as he was foolish. One of Nabal's servants hurried to her and told her that, in reply to David's greetings to Nabal, 'he hurled insults', but 'the men were very good to us . . . night and day they were a wall around us . . . see what you can do because disaster is hanging over our master and his whole household . . . no one can talk to him'.

Abigail lost no time. Without waiting to argue with her husband, she took not only the staple bread and mutton, but also raisins and pressed figs, which were rare delicacies in the desert, and sent her men on ahead with them to intercept David. She herself followed closely behind.

She met David and his men as they were coming down into a ravine, David threatening to cut off every male before the morning. As soon as she saw him, she bowed to the ground and asked him to put all the blame on her, since her husband was a fool. Then she put the argument in terms David could respect: 'The Lord has kept you in the past, my master, from bloodshed and from avenging yourself with your own hands.'

Those were the principles which had kept David from harming Saul and her words went straight to his heart. She respected him for his principles, how could he now deny them?

She used another argument. She also respected him as 'master'. He was 'the Lord's anointed' even if he was not yet king. 'When the Lord has done for my master everything he promised concerning him and appointed him leader over Israel, my master will not have on his conscience the staggering burden of needless bloodshed or of having avenged himself.'

Here, in the outback, was a woman who spoke to David in the spiritual language which appealed to his deep-rooted faith in God, a woman who believed in the destiny to which God had called him. She reminded him that he was no mere leader of an armed band, dealing out summary vengeance to all who crossed him, but one appointed by God to lead his nation.

David responded at once: 'Praise be to the LORD, the God of Israel, who has sent you today to meet me. May you be blessed for your good judgment and for keeping me from bloodshed this day and from avenging myself with my own hands.'

But, wise woman as she was, she also knew that David's band did need food. David accepted her gifts, and they parted.

Back at the ranch, she found Nabal very drunk, so she said nothing. When she told him next morning all that had happened, 'his heart failed him and he became like stone'. Ten days later he died from this stroke. David had allowed God to be the judge and God had judged.

That was not the end of the story. David had met a woman who was not only wise and courageous enough to stand up to him, but whose faith in God had, at that moment, been greater than his own. When he heard that Nabal had died, he sent a message asking her to become his wife. She responded at once, going back to David with his messengers. The feelings of respect were mutual. Her admiration for his faith and reputation was not just diplomatic, it was real. When, years later, David's sons quarrelled with him and with each other over the succession, we hear of no problem with the son of the wise and godly Abigail.

It was at this point, however, that David's polygamy began. Saul had given Michal, David's wife, to another man and, already, in her place, he had married Ahinoam of Jezreel, the mother of Amnon, who was David's first son and the first in the family to provoke his brothers into open conflict. So, with Abigail, David now had two wives. Although monogamy was not part of the civil law of Israel, every account we have of polygamy in Israel is a story of conflict in the family. Samuel's father had two wives and it had created friction and distress in the family. Jacob's two wives and two concubines had produced a family divided by jealousy and distrust, so if we are to judge by these accounts, monogamy seemed to be the ideal. If we are to judge David's wives by the behaviour of the sons they brought up, we can hardly believe that these wives were God's provision for David. So we could wish that David had waited for this one God-sent woman of faith and wisdom. Then he would surely have saved himself from the family troubles which overshadowed his old age.

David again spares Saul

After a while David ventured back towards Judah, but again he was betrayed to Saul by the Ziphites and, despite all he had said before, Saul once more brought his three thousand soldiers south down to the desert to look for David. Maybe it is not so surprising that the same people betrayed him again. Their first betrayal had made David their enemy and if Saul did not catch him, they thought they would be in danger from David. So one betrayal bred another.

When David's scouts reported that Saul and his men had arrived, David went out himself to look at their camp and spotted Saul and his commander Abner, both lying asleep, surrounded by sleeping soldiers. He asked his two companions whether they were prepared to go down with him through the army to Saul. Though it was evening and they knew their way, only Abishai his nephew volunteered for this very dangerous mission. When they arrived they found everyone fast asleep. Saul's spear was stuck in the ground by his head. Abishai offered to take the spear and kill Saul: 'Today God has given your enemy into your hands.'

David had allowed Saul to escape once and, despite all his fair words, Saul had come back again. Why let him go a second time, when God had clearly put a deep sleep on everyone and had put Saul at their mercy?

Once more, however, David would not let circumstances overrule principle. 'The LORD himself will strike him; either his time will come and he will die, or he will go into battle and perish. But the LORD forbid that I should lay a hand on the LORD's anointed.'

So they took the spear and the water jug at Saul's head and slipped away. All the soldiers remained in a deep sleep until David and Abishai had reached the top of a hill some distance away, with a wide space between them and the camp.

Then, in the dark, in the stillness of the dark night and within earshot, David called out to Abner, who was responsible for the king's safety, asking him to look first for Saul's spear and then his water jug and taunting him for his failure to guard the king. Saul recognized David's voice and called back.

David reached out to Saul's conscience. Again he said that he was innocent, as Saul had admitted last time. He said again that it was beneath Saul's dignity to chase him. He was not a bird of prey, but a partridge, which simply flew away from danger. If he, David, was in the wrong, then God would judge him. Again, he did not blame Saul himself, but his evil counsellors who had driven him from his share in the Lord's inheritance and had told him to go to serve other gods.

This time Saul really does seem to see his wrong. He no longer says, 'You are more righteous,' but 'I have sinned . . . I have acted like a fool and have erred greatly.' He begged David to come back and promised he would not try to harm him again. He ended, 'May you be blessed, my son David; you will surely triumph and do great things.'

That was to be their last encounter. Saul went back home and David went back to his men.

David returns to the Philistines

David was at a low ebb. Despite his great faith, despite all the times when God had preserved David from danger, first as shepherd, then as soldier and now as outlaw, David began to lose hope. He started to listen to his own fears and to forget God's care, and then he told himself that one day Saul would finally destroy him. No-one else had joined the six hundred and there seemed to his gloomy outlook to be no end to their hunted lives. Besides they had wives and families. Without consulting Gad or Abiathar, he concluded that it was best to go back to the Philistines; then Saul would stop searching for him.

So David, with his six hundred and their wives, including Ahinoam and Abigail, made their way westwards to Gath. This time David was not alone; he had six hundred experienced fighting men, who would be a useful addition to Achish's forces. David also, and wisely, suggested that he did not live in the royal city, making it clear that he was not ambitious to displace the other princes around the court. Instead David asked Achish whether he and his men could live in one of the country towns. Achish asked him to garrison Ziklag, a town on the border with both Judah and the Amalakites.

The Amalakites were one of the nations condemned by God for a wickedness which had gone so far that they were a peril to all around them. They had not been conquered by Joshua and Saul had been told by God, through Samuel, to attack them. Samuel's was a terrible message. 'I will punish the

Amalakites for what they did to Israel when they waylaid them as they came from Egypt. Now go, attack the Amalakites and totally destroy everything that belongs to them. Do not spare them; put to death men and women, children and infants, cattle and sheep, camels and donkeys.'

David believed in the reality of a God who had miraculously saved his people from the tyranny of the Pharaohs, had brought them through the Red Sea on dry land, had prevented the Amalakites from killing them all, had fed them and kept them clothed for forty years in the desert, had brought them dryshod across the Jordan and had delivered the mighty warriors of Canaan into their hands. There were signs enough that their God was the only God and that all Moses had taught in his five books about God the Creator was true. David knew also that God, who had protected David himself, the Lord whom his own experience taught him to trust, had given an authentic command, through Samuel, to destroy the Amalakites.

David also knew that because Saul spared the Amalakite king and the best of the flocks, God had finally rejected him as king over Israel. So David made raids on the Amalakites and spared nothing and no-one.

David, however, was almost certainly in the wrong. God had told Saul, through Samuel, to destroy the Amalakites, but he had not told David. God's last instructions to David had been to stay in the borders of Judah. David was also carrying out the raids with the side-objective of persuading Achish that he was raiding Judah. He hoped that Achish would think, as indeed he did, that David could be trusted by the Philistines because he had made himself offensive to his own people. Furthermore David was killing everyone, not because of God's commands about the Amalakites, but because he was afraid that survivors would live to tell the tale and that it would get back to Achish.

As a consequence of David's successful dishonesty, Achish asked him to join the Philistine army in a new attack on Israel. The Philistines, in this attack, marched a long way north, almost to the Jordan opposite Ephraim and David and his army marched in the rear. David was only saved from attacking his own people by the suspicion of the other Philistine commanders that David's men would change sides during the battle. 'How much better could he regain his master's favour than by taking the heads of our own men?' So Achish apologetically asked David to return. David, keeping up the pretence, asked Achish what he had done to offend him, but Achish insisted that they left at first light.

It was another consequence of David's actions, however, which was the most harrowing. After a three-day march back home to Ziklag, the six hundred found that the Amalakites had been there before them. The town had been destroyed by fire and all their wives and families had been taken captive, including Ahinoam and Abigail. It was David's lowest point because his men, in their distress, put all the blame on him and even talked of stoning him.

This disaster brought David back to God. He told Abiathar to bring the ephod and asked whether he should pursue the Amalakites and whether he would overtake them. God's answer was, 'Pursue them. You will certainly overtake them and succeed in the rescue.'

They needed this encouragement. The warrior band had been marching for six days, three days out and three days back, and the Amalakites might have gone anywhere. Two hundred of them went part of the way and had to stop from exhaustion. David told them to look after the baggage and four hundred went on.

Divine providence brought them to an Egyptian slave who had been taken ill and had been abandoned by the Amalakites. When he had had something to eat and drink he told them that, if they promised not to kill him or hand him back, he would lead them to the raiding band.

They found the Amalakites scattered around eating, drinking and having a great party. They far outnumbered David's men, but away out in the southern desert, with the Philistines and Israel battling in the far north, they evidently had not bothered with warning outposts. David's surprise attack must have cut down their numbers swiftly, but weary and desperate he and his men had to fight the rest of them for the next twenty-four

54

hours. Finally 'none of them got away except four hundred young men who rode off on camels and fled'.

David recovered everyone and everything and in addition they took all the plunder the Amalakites had taken on the other raids they had made on the Kerethites and on Judah. Those who had fought for twenty-four hours believed that they were entitled to the whole plunder, but David made it a rule that all, including those who guarded the baggage, should share alike. His authority had been restored and the rule was obeyed.

When they got back to Ziklag, he also, diplomatically, sent some of the plunder to the elders of Judah in all the places where he and his men had been. But nothing was sent to Keilah or to the Ziphites.

The end of the king

Meantime the Philistines and the Israelites confronted each other at Mount Gilboa. When Saul saw the Philistine army, he was terrified. He had rejected God and God had rejected him, so, though he himself had forbidden witchcraft, he went in disguise during the night to consult a witch, asking her to bring up Samuel from the dead to advise him.

This was a request to commit the sin of necromancy, specifically forbidden by Moses (Deuteronomy 18:11). It is argued that it was unlikely that God would allow Samuel to appear at a witch's summons. Although early church fathers believed that Samuel did appear, Tertullian, Jerome, Luther and Calvin believed that a demon impersonated Samuel. The apparition of an old man wearing a robe appeared out of the ground to the witch – but not to Saul – and, through the witch, told Saul that 'The LORD will hand over both Israel and you to the Philistines, and tomorrow you and your sons will be with me.'

It is argued that the real Samuel would have told Saul to repent and turn to God, that God gives hope to those who come to him and that it is the work of the devil to encourage despair and self-destruction. On the other hand, the text reads 'When the woman saw Samuel, she cried at the top of her voice and said to Saul "Why have you deceived me? You are Saul!"

. . . Then Saul knew it was Samuel . . . Samuel said to Saul "Why . . . ?" . . . Saul fell full length on the ground, filled with fear because of Samuel's words.' So, hesitant though we must be to disagree with Calvin and Luther, the text seems clear that it was Samuel, and the witch certainly met something quite different from the familiar spirit she expected.

In any case the effect of the message was to send Saul back to his army totally demoralized. The army of Israel was routed on Mount Gilboa and Jonathan and two of his brothers were killed. As the battle circled round him, Saul was wounded by an arrow. Saul's last thoughts were not of God but of his loss of dignity were he captured alive to be tortured by the Philistines and so he asked his armour-bearer to kill him. His armour-bearer rightly refused to kill his king, so Saul fell on his sword, committing suicide. When the army saw that the king was dead, they fled and the Israelites abandoned the towns on the west bank.

Saul's death brought to an end David's years as an outlaw.

3
King

David hears of the deaths of Saul and Jonathan

On the third day after David and the six hundred had returned
to Ziklag, an Amalakite came from Mount Gilboa and told them
that the Israelite army had been scattered and that Saul and
Jonathan were dead. David's first act was to mourn for Saul
and Jonathan; then he composed a beautiful lament for them,
with phrases which are still in use today,

> Tell it not in Gath,
>   proclaim it not in the streets
>   of Ashkelon.
> Saul and Jonathan –
>   in life they were loved and
>   gracious,
>   and in death they were not parted.
>
> How the mighty have fallen in battle!
>   Jonathan lies slain on your heights.
> I grieve for you, Jonathan my brother;
>   you were very dear to me.
> Your love for me was wonderful,
>   more wonderful than that of women.

The mourning for Saul was genuine. He had been David's
king, his father-in-law and father of his closest friend. Although
Saul had tried to kill David and had hounded him through the
crags and deserts, yet, when Saul was in his hands, David had
twice refused to take his life and had instead rebuked him with
great courtesy, treating him as an erring father. The lament,
in omitting mention of the injuries Saul had done him, forgave
them all.

He then called for the Amalakite who had brought the news
and who had also given David Saul's crown and bracelet.

The Amalakite had said that he had killed the fatally wounded king at his own request – evidently looking for some reward from David for despatching his enemy. David asked him, 'Why were you not afraid to lift your hand to destroy the Lord's anointed?'

Although Saul had asked his armour-bearer to kill him to prevent his falling alive into the hands of the Philistines, his armour-bearer had refused and Saul had taken his own life. But David knew nothing of that. He took the Amalakite at his word and ordered his immediate execution. David behaved like a leader, careful of public justice. And Saul's blood was not going to be on David's hands. There would be no breach with the house of Saul.

David anointed King of Judah in Hebron

There was no rush for the throne. Only 'in time' did David enquire of the Lord whether he should go up to one of the towns of Judah. The answer was that he should go up to Hebron. Hebron was a priests' city and a city of refuge, the capital of the tribe of Judah. He took his two wives, Ahinoam and Abigail, with him, and his friends and followers with their wives found homes in the villages around. In Hebron the elders of Judah anointed him king over Judah.

From Hebron, David sent messages to the men of Jabesh-Gilead who had, at great risk to themselves, rescued and buried the bodies of Saul and Jonathan and he promised to reward them. He also pointed out that, on Saul's death, the house of Judah had anointed him king over them. It was both a genuine and a politic message. But David needed more than politic messages before he was accepted outside Judah.

Mount Gilboa, where Saul had perished, was at the heart of the west bank, which all now lay under Philistine domination. Abner, Saul's cousin and commander of the defeated army, retreated from there beyond the Jordan and set up his headquarters at Mahanaim, on the east bank. He proclaimed one of Saul's remaining sons, Ish-Bosheth, as king. Abner was not going to quit without a fight.

Abner fights to keep the northern tribes

The fight came at the pool of Gibeon. Abner, representing the house of Saul, and Joab, for David, attempted to avoid civil war by agreeing to settle the issue by a series of single combats. 'Let's have some of the young men get up and fight hand to hand in front of us.' All twenty-four of the combatants, however, appear to have killed each other so single combat did not decide the issue. A fierce battle was then joined and Abner's forces were defeated, and fled. Asahel, Joab's brother, and one of David's 'three mighty men', chased Abner single-mindedly. Abner, who did not want to kill one of Joab's brothers, warned him off twice and, when he ignored the warnings, killed him by an unexpected backward blow with the sharp butt-end of his spear.

At evening the two armies halted. Abner appealed to Joab not to create a bitter feud by pursuit to the death, and Joab, knowing that David wanted a peaceful settlement, withdrew. Abner retreated over the Jordan with the loss of three hundred and sixty men and Joab and Abishai returned to Hebron, having buried Asahel in their home town of Bethlehem, with the loss of only twenty.

David took four more wives in Hebron and there were born to him the sons who were later to cause him such trouble: Amnon, Absalom and Adonijah. David should have known better. Moses had laid down that any future king of Israel, 'must not take many wives or his heart will be led astray'.

Absalom's mother was a princess, the daughter of the King of Geshur, north of Israel. It was clearly a dynastic marriage, but that does not excuse it.

Abner's position grew weaker. He was evidently not strong enough to recover the west bank and Ish-Bosheth seems to have been no help. Support gradually built up for David, but he would not allow Joab to press the advantage. Eventually this policy bore fruit. Seeing his support drifting away, and being provoked by Ish-Bosheth, Abner sent friendly messages to David. David made it a condition that Abner should return David's first wife, Saul's daughter, Michal, whom Saul had married off to another man. He may well have felt a genuine affection for Michal, who had saved his life from Saul's hands, but to re-establish his marriage links to the house of Saul would obviously help the union of the kingdoms. Abner obliged, removed Michal from her tearful second husband and, after discussions with the elders of Israel – 'for some time you have wanted David as your king; now do it!' – came to Hebron with a retinue, promising to bring Israel over to David. David gave him a great feast and sent him away to do as he had promised.

Abner's murder

When Joab, returning from an expedition, was told of the reconciliation, he was, like any soldier, deeply suspicious of a political settlement and told David that Abner was not to be trusted: 'You know Abner the son of Ner; he came to deceive you and observe your movements and find out everything you are doing.' Behind that advice was the fear that the general who brought over all the rest of the tribes would naturally take Joab's present place as the second man in the kingdom. So he decided to take matters into his own hands. He sent a messenger to Abner to bring him back and then taking him aside, as if to give him a message, he murdered him.

According to the law of Moses, Joab should have been executed for the murder of Abner, but he claimed that he had acted as an 'avenger of blood' for the death of his brother, Asahel. Although the 'avenger of blood' was recognized under the law, this was not a valid plea, since Asahel had been killed in battle. But the plea was made by the surviving commander of the army, whose surviving brother was also his second in command. David admitted that though he was the recently anointed king 'these sons of Zeruiah are too strong for me'. He left judgment in God's hands, but he did not forgive or forget. When handing over power at the end of his life, he reminded his successor of this piece of unfinished business. Solomon waited until Joab had once more put himself in the wrong and this famous but flawed soldier finally died by the sword. David was not the first ruler, and certainly not the last, to be at the mercy of army chiefs, but David knew and respected God's law. Justice was not set aside, simply deferred.

Meantime David, both from genuine feeling and to limit the political damage, distanced himself from Joab's crime as far as he could. He washed his hands publicly from the guilt of Abner's blood, 'I and my kingdom are for ever innocent before the LORD concerning the blood of Abner the son of Ner.'

David ordered the whole court, including Joab, into mourning. He put the guilt of Abner's blood on Joab and delivered a eulogy on Abner. He walked behind the bier, wept at the tomb and delivered a funeral oration,

> 'Should Abner have died as the lawless die?
> Your hands were not bound, your feet were not
>   fettered.
> You fell as one falls before wicked men.'

Coming home, he fasted for the rest of the day and told his men, 'Do you not realize that a prince and a great man is fallen in Israel this day.'

David's efforts were successful in persuading the people that he had nothing to do with Abner's death and, in the event, they did not stop the other tribes from coming over to him. Indeed the eventual union was probably the stronger for their not being delivered by a great leader, but coming by a genuine popular movement.

Formally Ish-Bosheth was still king of the northern tribes. But he had been a puppet of Abner without any strength of his own and could not stand in the way of public feeling.

There was another descendant of Saul, Jonathan's son Mephibosheth, but he had been lamed as a child when dropped by his nurse and, since a lame king could not lead his people into battle, he was not considered a possible successor.

One day David was confronted by two of Ish-Bosheth's soldiers, carrying his head, and saying, 'Here is the head of Ish-Bosheth, son of Saul, your enemy, who tried to take your life. This day the LORD has avenged my lord the king against Saul and his offspring.'

David told them that he had put to death the man who reported that he had killed the dying Saul at his own request and added, 'How much more – when wicked men have killed an innocent man in his own house and on his own bed – should I not now demand his blood from your hand!'

So they were executed and the head of Ish-Bosheth was buried in Abner's tomb in Hebron.

David anointed King over all Israel

Then the tribes of Israel came to David in Hebron, represented by several thousand soldiers from each tribe, including those from Zebulun and Napthali in the far north. They brought their own provisions, stayed three days and said, 'We are your own flesh and blood. In the past, while Saul was king over us, you were the one who led Israel on their military campaigns. And the LORD said to you, "You shall shepherd my people Israel, and you shall become their ruler." ' So they anointed David king and 'There was great joy in Israel.'

David had reigned seven years in Hebron, which is at the southern end of the long ridge between the Mediterranean and the Jordan valley and a long way from the northern tribes. He now looked for a more strategic capital and set his sights on a rocky citadel further north along the same central ridge. It was on the borders of Judah and Benjamin, not too far from the tribes on the east bank of the Jordan and flanking the tribes on the west bank, now under Philistine domination.

The capture of Jerusalem from the Jebusites

David's only problem was that the Benjamites, who had been badly damaged in the civil war before the time of Samuel, had allowed the former inhabitants, the Jebusites, to take over the citadel. It was surrounded on three sides by deep ravines and was said to be impregnable. But it was typical of David the soldier that he wanted to capture his own capital and not take it over from someone else. He promised the command of the newly united army to whoever could take it – certainly one sure way of settling that argument.

David told his men that the only way in was by the water-shaft, a tunnel and vertical shaft (still to be seen today) which connected the citadel with the Gihon spring just to the east of the city wall. It cannot have been an easy job, since the tunnel is narrow and the vertical ascent has to be made as a rock-climber today goes up a 'chimney', bracing his body against the opposite wall. And, at the top, the surprise had to be complete. But, under the daring leadership of Joab, it was done, the citadel of Zion was captured and Jerusalem, the City of David, was established as the national capital.

David now had a fortress right on the southern flank of the west bank, which the Philistines had dominated since their victory on Mount Gilboa. If they were to hold their gain, they had to dislodge him quickly and crush the newly fledged union. They had defeated one king of a united Israel and they did not want another. The Philistine tactics were bold.

Attacks by Philistines

They came up silently through the defiles and suddenly spread out in the valley of Rephaim, only a few miles south-west of Jerusalem. David went at once to man a key defensive stronghold and then faced the agonizing decision; should he hold back until he could muster Israel in force or should he attack with the much smaller numbers immediately available to him in Judah? If he waited, the Philistines could do great damage in Judah, the heart of his kingdom, and destroy the trust he had to create as the new leader capable of defending the united kingdom. A quick attack, however, could find him outnumbered and soon defeated.

David asked the Lord whether he should go up against them and, to make doubly sure, he asked whether, if he did, the Lord would hand them over to him. The reply came, 'Go and I will surely hand the Philistines over to you.' David needed that encouragement and made a sudden frontal attack, like 'waters bursting out'. Saul, faced with a similar situation, had seen his men melt away in fear, and maybe the Philistines were taken by surprise at the early and confident action. Maybe they had underestimated the battle-hardened veterans under Joab and the military training they had been able to give to other men of Judah in the seven years since David became king in Hebron. They were also far from base and David had his capital just behind him. Whatever the reason, the Philistines ran, abandoning their idols on the field. David, showing his horror of idolatry, burnt the wooden images.

Clearly the Philistines could hardly believe what had happened to them, because they came back along the same route, probably in greater numbers, and spread out once more in the valley of Rephaim. David again asked the Lord for guidance. This time the Lord told him to circle round behind them and, 'As soon as you hear the sound of marching in the tops of the balsam trees, move quickly, because that will mean that the Lord has gone out in front of you to strike the Philistine army.'

Philistine support-forces were coming up through the narrow defile to make sure that David's smaller army could not defeat them again. It was a bold move to come right up to David's capital, but even bolder, having shown themselves in force in the valley of Rephaim, to continue to put the support-troops through the narrow defile behind them. They must have reckoned that David would not dare to allow the Philistine main force to be between him and Jerusalem. But they had reckoned without the swift and silent movement of those former outlaws, David and Joab, or the boldness of men who knew their own ground – and who were accustomed to trust their lives to God's battle-plan.

As the marching support-troops came abreast, David's men pounced from above. Trapped in the defile, the Philistines would have been defenceless, while up in the valley the main force realized that disaster had struck behind them, cutting them off. The record reads, 'David . . . struck down the Philistines all the way from Gideon to Gezer.'

David did not allow the Philistines to recover. We read, 'David defeated the Philistines and subdued them, and he took Metheg Ammah [this can be translated as "the metropolis"] from the control of the Philistines.'

We hear of no more trouble for a long time from David's western flank.

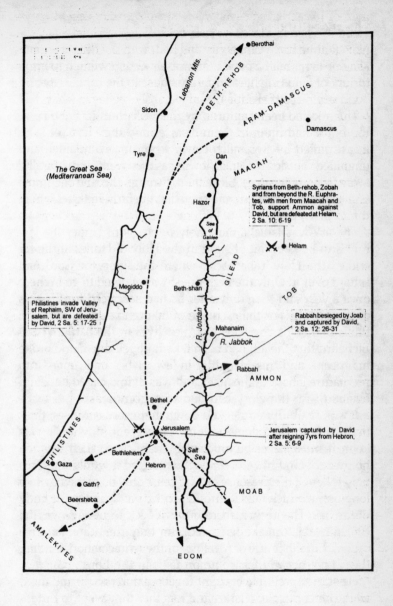

Berothai

Sidon

Lebanon Mts.

BETH-REHOB

ARAM-DAMASCUS

Damascus

Tyre

The Great Sea
(Mediterranean Sea)

Dan

MAACAH

Hazor

Syrians from Beth-rehob, Zobah
and from beyond the R. Euphrates, with men from Maacah and
Tob, support Ammon against
David, but are defeated at Helam,
2 Sa. 10: 6-19

Sea
of
Galilee

Helam

GILEAD

Megiddo

Beth-shan

TOB

R. Jordan

Philistines invade Valley
of Rephaim, SW of Jeru-
salem, but are defeated
by David, 2 Sa. 5: 17-25

Mahanaim

R. Jabbok

Rabbah besieged by Joab
and captured by David,
2 Sa. 12: 26-31

Rabbah

AMMON

Bethel

PHILISTINES

Jerusalem

Jerusalem captured by David
after reigning 7yrs from Hebron,
2 Sa. 5: 6-9

Bethlehem

Salt
Sea

Gaza

Hebron

Gath?

MOAB

Beersheba

AMALEKITES

EDOM

The wars of David's reign

The ark of God brought to Jerusalem

Now that he had a capital city and had, with the help of Hiram, King of Tyre, built a palace for himself, David wanted to bring the ark of God from its temporary house to the capital city and build a temple there for it.

The ark had been captured by the Philistines in the time of Eli, but it had brought them disaster and they had set it on a cart pulled by two milch cows, who, unaccompanied and unguided, headed for Israel 'lowing as they went', unnaturally, away from their calves. Since then, through the rule of Samuel and the reign of Saul, it had stayed at the farm in Israel where it had arrived.

The ark was Israel's most holy possession. Under the law it was to be kept out of sight in the Holy of Holies at the far end of the Holy Tabernacle, where the 'glory of God' had settled over it. Only the high priest was allowed to go in there once a year and then only after he had sacrificed for the sins of the people. For the sacrilege of taking the ark to fight the Philistines, Eli's two sons lost their lives in the battle. When Eli heard that the ark had been taken, he fell down and broke his neck, and his daughter-in-law, who had gone into premature labour at the news and was dying, called her child Ichabod, 'for the glory had departed from Israel'.

It was an absolute rule, laid down in the law of Moses, that, in moving the ark along with the desert tent in which it was kept, it must never be touched by hand and, such was the holiness of God, that anyone who touched it would die. This holy token of the presence of God must only be carried by two long poles, which held it through sockets attached to the body of the ark. David wanted to bring it back to his new capital city in order to make Jerusalem not only the administrative capital, but the centre of worship for the whole nation, binding them together in their common faith in the Lord.

He started well. He brought together thirty thousand men, all the chief people in Israel and together they went to Kiriath Jearim, where the ark had returned to Israel from the Philistines. But the sons of the farmer who had kept the ark had arranged to move it away in the same manner that it had arrived from the Philistines, on a clumsy ox cart, and they forgot that the oxen had brought it there without any human direction. As the oxen stumbled, one of them, Uzzah, reached out his hand to steady the ark, and, as Moses had warned of anyone touching the ark, he fell dead.

No-one in the thirty thousand can then have been in doubt that the ark was holy and that the God who fought their battles for them was a being of awesome power who required that they kept, to the letter, all the laws he had given them.

David was horrified that a venture which was meant to have crowned all his achievements had come to grief so disastrously and he refused to take the ark any further. God, however, wanted the ark to go to Jerusalem and, after a few months, it was reported to David that the farm where he had now left it had received many signs of God's favour. So he went down and set out with the ark carried on poles by the Levites, as the law required. After six paces he offered a sacrifice of atonement and then the procession went on to the City of David, with great rejoicing, singing and playing of trumpets, cymbals, lyres and harps and the sounding of rams' horns.

In the words of Psalm 68:24–26,

> Your procession has come into view, O God,
>> the procession of my God and
>>> King into the sanctuary.
> In front are the singers, after them
>> the musicians;
>> with them are the maidens
>> playing tambourines.
> Praise God in the great congregation;
>> praise the LORD in the assembly
>>> of Israel.

And Psalm 132:7–8,

> Let us go to his dwelling-place;
>> let us worship at his footstool –

arise, O LORD, and come to your
resting place,
you and the ark of your might.

We read, 'David, wearing a linen ephod, danced before the
LORD with all his might, while he and the entire house of Israel
brought up the ark of the LORD with shouts and the sound of
trumpets' (2 Samuel 6:14–15).

They put the ark in a tent which David had made ready and
David sacrificed burnt offerings before the Lord. Then he gave
everyone in the great crowd food and went home to bless his
family, full of happiness.

A sour-faced Michal came out to meet him before he could
set foot in his house. Michal's pride as a princess of a royal
house had been offended by his informal behaviour and she
scolded him because his dancing in a linen ephod in front of
all the young girls was vulgar and unbecoming to a king.

David reminded her that God had appointed him ruler over
the Lord's people rather than her father or anyone from his
house and 'I will celebrate before the Lord,' he said, and he
added that he would be even more undignified, but would be
held in honour by the girls of whom she spoke.

Then we are told that Michal had no children to the day of
her death.

God's covenant with David

David was now established, with his great men and officers
of state around him and the ark in Jerusalem, but felt that there
was one thing more to be done. He said to Nathan the prophet,
'Here I am, living in a palace of cedar, while the ark of God
remains in a tent.'

He was grateful for all God's goodness to him, and wanted
to show it by building a temple to God's glory. Nathan told
him to do whatever he had in mind. Nathan, however, had
not asked the Lord and that night the Lord sent him back to
David with a different message.

God told David that he was not to build him a house. He
had moved with his people 'from one tent site to another, from

68

one dwelling place to another'. He had never asked for a house of cedar. Other things were more important. He would make David's name 'like the names of the greatest men on earth. And I will provide a place for my people Israel and will plant them so that they can have a home of their own and no longer be disturbed.'

God has more to say to David

It might have seemed to David then that he had come to the end of his military career and that the territorial bounds of Israel were now set. There were still hostile nations round about, however, and David had battles still to fight before Israel was free from attack. And God would reward him. David wanted to build God a house, but God would build him a house instead. He would establish David's kingdom and his dynasty and one of his own sons would build God's house. Then the prophecy seems to slide from the immediate to the far future, with the first hint of the Messiah who was to come from the house of David: 'I will set him over my house and my kingdom for ever; his throne will be established for ever.' That can hardly refer to the line of kings which was to follow for several hundred years; the promise is clearly of a different kind of throne and kingdom.

David's response was humble, grateful, trusting and had great spiritual insight. It could not have been bettered. 'Who am I, O Sovereign LORD and what is my family that you have brought me this far? . . . How great you are, O Sovereign LORD! There is no-one like you and there is no God but you . . . Your words are trustworthy . . . you, O Sovereign LORD, have spoken, and with your blessing the house of your servant will be blessed for ever.

War with Moab

David seems next to have turned to his east flank, to the Moabites on the other side of the Dead Sea. While an outlaw, David had committed his father and mother to the King of Moab, being related through Jesse's Moabite grandmother Ruth. So it seems odd that he should have marched against

Moab. But all the peoples round Israel had attacked Israel whenever she seemed to be weak and it may be that, while David was occupied with the Philistines in the west, Moab on the eastern frontier had taken advantage.

In this war we come, for the first time in David's story, to the full horror of these ancient wars. When a modern army surrenders, it gives up its arms and, after the war is over, the disarmed prisoners are sent home. Without guns, aircraft and missiles, they are impotent. But in ancient war it was only too easy for a defeated nation to rearm. The bows and arrows, which were the main weapons of the hill people, cost little and slings and stones cost nothing at all. So long as the enemy had able-bodied men, they could attack again and again.

Prisoners were only taken if they could be enslaved, transported or otherwise made harmless for the future. Small nations, however, had nowhere to transport prisoners and slaves. In a small country they could be over the border in a day. Leniency lay in killing only some of those captured and releasing others to go back home to fight against you another day.

Moses had laid down the law for Israel (Deuteronomy 20:10–13):

> When you march up to attack a city, make its people
> an offer of peace. If they accept and open their gates,
> all the people in it shall be subject to forced labour and
> shall work for you. If they refuse to make peace and
> they engage you in battle, lay siege to that city. When
> the LORD your God delivers it into your hand, put to
> the sword all the men in it.

David was a good deal more lenient, sending home over a third of the Moabite soldiers.

So-called Christian countries have, in two wars this century, killed fifty million of each other's citizens, armed and civilian. And if we think we would not do that again, we should reflect that a central policy of the NATO alliance was the threat of massive retaliation on open cities with nuclear weapons, which

would have killed millions of innocent women and children.
So we cannot be too sure that, faced with defeat and death,
we would have been more lenient than David.

Between the conquest of Canaan by Joshua and the time of
Saul and David, as recorded in the book of Judges, Israel had
been attacked time and again by its neighbours. These attackers
included the Sidonians from the coast north-east of Israel, the
Hivites from the Lebanon mounts, Aram from the north, Moab
from the land across the Dead Sea in the east, Hazor and
Midian, the Amalakites from the south-east, the Ammonites
from the east across the Jordan, south of Israel's own trans-
Jordan territory of Gilead, and the Philistines. There was no
peace in the area. David's contribution to his people was to
establish a peace not only within Israel's borders, but beyond
them, a peace which lasted for the rest of his long reign and
all the reign of his successor. The tribute he took from the kings
under his protection was a relatively small price to pay for the
end of bloody tribal warfare.

David's fighting men

To fight the kingdoms which surrounded Israel, David needed
an army which was bigger and more organized than the force
which twice defeated the Philistines outside Jerusalem. No
small country could afford a standing army. The crops had to
be sown and reaped, the sheep needed shepherds. So the army
was organized on the basis of a month's call-up in a year, which
according to the Chronicles (1 Chronicles 27) gave twenty-four
thousand men under arms each month, under a different
general for each successive month. It also seems likely, from
the numbers of soldiers who came to Hebron to make David
king over Israel, that each tribe would have been responsible
for arranging its own contribution.

Under this flexible arrangement, there would have been a
month's training if there were no campaign, a standing army
for an emergency, and the possibility of calling out a much
bigger trained reserve army if it were needed.

At the core of the army were the six hundred veterans from
David's time as an outlaw, men who knew how to use the

countryside, how to make long forced marches, appearing suddenly when no-one expected them, men who had done a hundred ambushes and who were skilled in the use of every weapon. No doubt these men trained the new army, stiffened it and led it into battle.

At the heart of his core of six hundred were thirty named soldiers, the 'mighty men' who had proved themselves with David when he was an outlaw. They were not all from Israel. There was Zelek the Ammonite and Uriah the Hittite. Asahel, brother of Joab, killed by Abner, had been in this group of thirty. Then there were the Three whose exploits were even more exceptional. Abishai, the surviving brother of Joab was, though not a member, chief of the Three. The Three had broken through Saul's lines to draw water from the well at Bethlehem when David in his thirst had said that he longed for it. (David, who was horrified that they had taken him at his word and had risked their lives, would not drink it but poured it out, sacrificially, on the ground.)

Beniah, the son of Jehoiada, was chief of the guard and Joab was commander in chief of the army. It was not just a brave army, it was organized, disciplined and trained and, under David's inspiration and leadership, absolutely dedicated.

War in the north

We next hear of David in the far north, fighting Hadadezer, son of Rehob, King of Zobah 'as he went to restore his control along the Euphrates River'. The Kingdom of Zobah is said to have extended over much of what is present-day Syria, with its centre somewhere between the modern Aleppo and Damascus. Tou, King of Hamath, in the eastern valley of present-day Lebanon, running down to Israel's border (the Beka Valley), had been at war with this aggressive and dangerous power and was David's ally.

David won a remarkable victory. For the first time he captured chariots, charioteers and horses in their thousands. It may be that Hadadezer, used to using chariots and horses on the Syrian plains, had been lured to higher ground where he was at a disadvantage against David's army. Or it may be that David appeared unexpectedly from the valley kingdom of his ally Tou, the northern end of which emerged near the heart of Hadadezer's kingdom. Three arguments support this thesis.

Firstly, it is likely that David would not be so far north (one hundred miles north of Israel's border) unless an ally, feeling threatened, had asked for him.

Secondly, it was a mark of David's tactics to march swiftly and appear unexpectedly. Surprise would be necessary against the horses and chariots.

Thirdly, he went on to defeat the Arameans who had come to Hadadezer's aid. To have defeated Hadadezer first, David must already be north of the Arameans and could only have got there through Hamath.

David hamstrung all but a hundred of the chariot horses and burnt the chariots. He did not take the horses as booty because of Samuel's warnings to Israel against allowing their kings to keep great and expensive military establishments – and horses were very expensive for a small country.

The Jewish king returned to the southern border, which Abishai had been defending against the Edomites while the main army was in the north and 'became famous after he returned from striking down eighteen thousand Edomites in the Valley of Salt'.

There remained one powerful neighbour, Ammon, just across the Jordan from Jericho. Saul had won his spurs in rescuing Ramoth-Gilead from Nahash, King of Ammon, who had threatened to put out one eye of each of the defenders. But, perhaps because Saul had been opposed to David, the King of Ammon had been David's friend when he was an outlaw. So when he died, David sent ambassadors to offer commiserations to his son and heir. Now, however, David was a powerful neighbour and the advisers of the new King Hanun suggested to him that David's ambassadors had really been sent to spy out the ground.

A wise king might have doubted the advice, but even had he believed it, he would have received the ambassadors and sent them with fulsome compliments speedily on their way. Instead, in an act of appalling folly, Hanon cut off half their beards and cut their clothes up to their buttocks before sending them back.

The beard, in those days, was the sign of manhood and dignity and there could be no worse insult. David, careful of their feelings, told them to stay in Jericho until their beards had grown again. Hanun, realizing the full impact of what he had done, prepared for war, sending to Aram for help, for which he paid heavily.

David, who did not want the war on his own territory, took the initiative and the armies met outside the Ammonite capital. The Ammonites stayed in front of their walls, which was not very brave, and the Arameans kept further out in the country where they had room to manoeuvre their chariots and cavalry.

Joab took advantage of this division of the opposing forces and put his army between the other two, leaving Abishai to hold the line against the weaker Ammonites, while he commanded the major part of the army against the Arameans. The brothers had the internal lines and could come to each other's help if either got under too much pressure. On the other hand, they could easily have been surrounded if the battle went badly against them. It was a bold move, but the venture succeeded.

Joab's men held their own against the Aramean mercenaries, who cannot have been too inspired by the way in which the Ammonites, whom they had come to help, kept so close to the gate into the city. Joab's men were fighting for a cause in which they all believed, and for a commander and a king whom they trusted. They put the Arameans to flight, whereupon the Ammonites poured back into the city and closed the gates.

The Arameans had not been fighting their own cause, but they could not ignore the effect their loss had on their power and influence and they gathered their forces to re-establish their authority, led by King Hadadezer, who had his previous defeat to avenge. David did not wait for them. He went north and met them at Helam, east of Gilead. Again he probably arrived unexpectedly, throwing this clumsy coalition into confusion

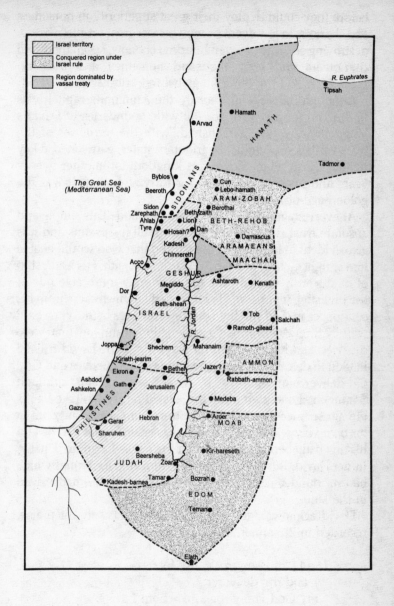

David's kingdom

before they could deploy their great superiority in horsemen and chariots. In any event he won his last great set-piece battle, destroying an army of seven hundred chariots, seven thousand charioteers and forty thousand horsemen and infantry. Hadadezer and the other kings became tributaries of David.

Although the siege of Rabbah, the Ammonite capital, was to drag on for a year or so, the wide boundaries of David's kingdom were now established, with the territories of the twelve tribes surrounded by tributary states, garrisoned at key points. David reigned over this kingdom for another twenty years and his son, Solomon, for forty after that. It was the golden age of Israel.

At every stage, David had trusted in God. This simple and absolute trust is reflected throughout all his psalms and it is also evident in his actions. He trusted that God would enable him to fight Goliath and God rewarded his faith. His leadership of Saul's army turned back the seemingly inexorable tide of the Philistine invasions. He had a daring which came from his confidence in God and the Lord rewarded his faith. When Saul wilfully threw away David's leadership, he and Jonathan were defeated and killed. When he was an outlaw, David trusted in God to deliver him from the hands of his enemies and God did deliver him. Saul was in his power twice and, although Samuel had anointed him king, David refused to take Saul's life himself, leaving it to God to bring him to the kingdom in his own way and time. His trust was again repaid and he and his tiny band of outlaws took over the whole kingdom. Finally, under David, Israel was delivered from all the enemies which had surrounded it for the hundreds of years since it had arrived in the land.

David acknowledges all of this in a great song of praise, recorded in 2 Samuel 22.

> The LORD is my rock, my fortress
>   and my deliverer;
>   my God is my rock, in whom I
>   take refuge,
>   my shield and the horn of my salvation.

He is my stronghold, my refuge and
   my saviour –
  from violent men you save me.
I call to the LORD, who is worthy of praise,
  and I am saved from my enemies.

He reached down from high
   and took hold of me;
  he drew me out of deep waters.
He rescued me from my powerful enemy,
  from my foes who were too
   strong for me.
They confronted me in the day of my disaster,
  but the LORD was my support.

With your help I can advance
   against a troop;
  with my God I can scale a wall.

He makes my feet like the feet of a deer;
  he enables me to stand on the heights.
He trains my hand for the battle;
  my arms can bend a bow of bronze.

You armed me with strength for the battle;
  you made my adversaries bow at my feet.

People I did not know are subject to me;
  and foreigners come cringing to me;
  as soon as they hear me, they obey me.
They lose heart;
  they come trembling from their strongholds.

He is the God who avenges me,
  who puts the nations under me,
  who sets me free from my enemies.
You exalted me above my foes;
  from violent men you rescued me.

Therefore I will praise you,
  O LORD, among the nations;
  I will sing praises unto your name.
He gives his king great victories;
  he shows unfailing kindness to his anointed,
  to David and his descendants for ever.

4
Trouble

Saul's family

David had sworn to Jonathan that he would look after his family, so when his wars seemed to be drawing to a conclusion, he sent to see whether there was anyone left of Saul's family to whom he could show kindness for Jonathan's sake. He was told that Jonathan's crippled son was in the house of Makir, son of Ammiel in Lo Debar, a town in Gilead, east of the River Jordan. So David sent for him and restored all the land which belonged to Saul, made him a member of his own court in Jerusalem, and gave him Ziba, a former servant of Saul's household, to look after his property. But Saul had left a more troublesome legacy.

Under the leadership of Joshua, successor to Moses, Israel had, hundreds of years earlier, crossed the River Jordan, and invaded and occupied the land of Canaan, where they now lived. Joshua was under divine instruction not to make treaties of peace with any of the idolatrous Canaanite tribes. But the Gibeonites, a branch of the Ammonites, came to him in worn clothing, pretending that they were from a distant people. Without further enquiry, he made a treaty with them. Though he soon discovered his mistake, he was obliged to keep to his word and the Gibeonites have lived with Israel, in a servile position, but at peace, over the centuries since then.

Despite this long-standing agreement, Saul had, without provocation, massacred the Gibeonites – a gross crime, for which no-one had been punished and which Israel seemed to have forgotten.

God had not forgotten, however, and he sent a famine for three successive years. David felt that it must be a message from God to Israel so he enquired of God and God replied, 'It is on account of Saul and his blood-stained house: it is because he put the Gibeonites to death.'

David summoned the survivors of the massacre and asked

them what amends he should make. The Gibeonites asked for the deaths of seven members of Saul's family; they had no demand to make against the people of Israel. It is probable that, as with Saul's massacre of the high priest and all his family, no Israelite could be found to carry it out. As Doeg the Edomite had murdered the priests, so Saul probably called on a few of his family to carry out the illegal slaughter of the helpless Gibeonites. God's command spoke of Saul 'and his blood-stained house'.

David chose two sons of Saul's concubine Rizpah, whose position, like that of their mother, must have depended entirely on Saul's whim. He also chose the five sons of Adriel, son of Barzillai the Meholathite, to whom Saul had given his elder daughter Merab instead of giving her to David as he had promised. They seem, too, to be a family exceptionally obliged to Saul and likely to have done as he asked. Mephibosheth, son of Jonathan, was under David's oath of protection and it is most unlikely that anyone from Jonathan's house would have countenanced such a massacre.

The Gibeonites accepted these seven as the proper members of Saul's house to be held responsible for the crime and David handed them over for execution.

The law of Moses states, 'Fathers shall not be put to death for their children, nor children put to death for their fathers; each is to die for his own sin' (Deuteronomy 24:16).

So we do not rely on circumstantial evidence alone for the belief that those executed were themselves responsible for the massacre. God does not break his own laws. He called for justice and, after the seven were executed, he ended the famine as his sign that his justice, which required that each should suffer for his or her own sin, had been satisfied.

David's marriages

By the time he had established his capital in Jerusalem, David had four wives: Michal, Saul's daughter, Ahinoam of Jezreel, mother of Amnon, Abigail and Maacah of Geshur, mother of Absalom and Tamar. To these were added other wives in Jerusalem. David, unlike his immediate forbears, Boaz, Obed and Jesse, had become a polygamist. He was not the first or the last in the history of Israel; but in every recorded case polygamy had brought trouble.

In polygamous marriages, no one wife has the rights which only monogamy can give, no one wife has the security to say what needs to be said to the husband without fear of disfavour. Furthermore, no one wife has the right to sort out quarrels among the children and bring unity into the family.

In David's case, he had become accustomed, in addition, to taking a woman if he wanted her. Therefore he was unaccustomed to the close companionship of one wife with whom he naturally shared all his hopes, fears and troubles, who had a natural right to his company, who would be there to sense that something was wrong and to lead him gently round a dangerous corner. Instead David's wives, including the wise Abigail, must, like the wives of any heathen king, wait to be summoned and must acknowledge the right of their husband to add another to their number.

The crisis of middle life

David, up to this point, had had a rough life. He had been a shepherd in the hills, a soldier, an outlaw, running for his life, a king fighting not just for his own life but also for the life of his people and now, at last, he could see peace and rest in the offing. The final formidable foe, the Ammonites, had been conquered and all that was needed now was to besiege and capture their capital city.

It must have been a powerful temptation to rest on his laurels and to leave this last siege to Joab. But it was the wrong decision. He was already too dependent on Joab. He was still asking all his comrades of a hundred fights to risk their lives while he stayed at home. Additionally, the siege of the Ammonite capital was a tough and lengthy business. Duty still called.

The luxury of the palace reached out its tentacles, the disciplines of army life were lifted, and middle-aged softness began to creep in. With all his closest friends away at the siege, his pattern of life suddenly changed and 'the devil found work for idle hands to do'.

In this idle moment, David went up to the roof of his palace. The roof of the new palace would have been higher than those of the surrounding houses. Where women had bathed out of sight of the street and, behind a wall, out of sight of their neighbours, they could now be seen from the palace roof. Was that the first time David had discovered this or was this perhaps why he was on the roof? If so, he would not be the first or the last good man to have 'accidentally' put himself in the way of temptation. Whether by accident or not, David saw a beautiful woman bathing on top of her house and he wanted her.

God's warning

God does not like to see a faithful servant fall into temptation and he will often give a chance to escape before it is too late. God gave David a last-minute chance. He did not at first send for the woman he had seen. He enquired who she was. The report came back that she was 'Bathsheba . . . the wife of Uriah the Hittite'. That reply should have stopped David in his tracks. Uriah was not only a leader in David's army, he was one of the Thirty, the elite band who had been with David when they were all outlaws together, always on the run, always fighting for their lives and owing their lives to the absolute trust and loyalty which bound them together. They were a group of which legends are made, the nucleus of the army who fought for the kingdom after Saul's death. They fought the Philistines and then all of Israel's traditional enemies, and were, even now, in front of the walls of Rabbah. How could David take the wife of any of his soldiers who was away at battle, but how, especially, could he take the wife of one of his closest and most trusted companions?

David's adultery

Yet David sent for Bathsheba and took her. There comes a point when blind lust sweeps all before it. Loyalty, friendship, calculation of consequences and plain prudence are all tramped down in a rush for what we want. That is why society puts up barriers to slow us down before we get to that point. But there were no barriers for a king. Bathsheba perhaps could have resisted. But when King David commanded your presence, it was natural to obey and, once inside the palace, it would have been hard to resist.

The attempted cover-up

Within a short time Bathsheba sent a note to David to say, 'I am pregnant'. David knew that unless he acted quickly his adultery with the wife of one of Israel's heroes would be discovered. So he asked for Uriah to be sent back to Jerusalem to make a report on the siege, expecting that he would go home and sleep with his wife and that David's paternity of the child would never be discovered.

Uriah came, but he did not go home to his wife after seeing David. Instead he slept at the entrance of the palace with David's servants. Uriah's answer, when David asked him why he had not gone home, can be taken as an implied rebuke. 'The ark and Israel and Judah are staying in tents, and my master Joab and my Lord's men are camped in the open fields. How could I go to my house and eat and drink and lie with my wife? As surely as I live I will not do such a thing!'

Desperately, David asked him to stay one more day and then made him drunk; but sober or drunk, Uriah would not change his mind. David now stooped to the lowest deed in his whole life. He wrote to Joab, sending the sealed letter with Uriah. The letter read, 'Put Uriah in the front line where the fighting is fiercest. Then withdraw from him so that he will be struck down and die.'

The murder of Uriah

Joab might have chosen to ignore the letter. He too had an obligation to this close and loyal comrade and it would not have been the first time that he had ignored David's commands. But obedience to this command would make a fundamental change in the balance of moral authority between king and commander. Joab might have killed Abner, but it was David who would have killed Uriah. David would be brought down to Joab's level and could no longer check his ruthlessness. If it suited him, Joab could threaten to expose David and could alienate him from the leaders of the army, who until then had owed a stronger allegiance to David than they did to Joab.

So it was that Uriah the Hittite, one of the famous 'thirty mighty men' went to his death at the most strongly defended section of the wall of Rabbah. Joab put a note of his death in the next despatch to David. When Bathsheba heard of her husband's death, she went into mourning; but after the time of mourning was over, David married her and she bore him a son.

God's judgment on David

David might try to hide his adultery and act of murder from other people, but he could not hide them from God. Nathan the prophet came to see David. He told him a story of a rich man who had a very large number of sheep and cattle and a poor man who had 'nothing except one little ewe lamb that he had bought. He raised it, and it grew up with him and his children. It shared his food, drank from his cup and even slept in his arms. It was like a daughter to him.' But, continued Nathan, when a traveller came to the rich man, he spared his own huge flock and killed the poor man's ewe lamb for a meal.

David was furious. 'As surely as the LORD lives, the man who did this deserves to die. He must pay for that lamb four times over, because he did such a thing and had no pity.'

Nathan said, 'You are the man! This is what the Lord God of Israel says, ''I anointed you king over Israel, and I delivered you from the hand of Saul. I gave your master's house to you, and your master's wives into your arms. I gave you the house of Israel and Judah. And if all this had been too little, I would have given you even more. Why did you despise the word of the Lord by doing what is evil in his eyes? You struck down Uriah the Hittite with the sword and took his wife to be your own. You killed him with the sword of the Ammonites. Now, therefore, the sword shall never depart from your house, because you despised me and took the wife of Uriah the Hittite to be your own . . . Out of your own household I am going to bring calamity upon you.'' '

It is to David's credit that he repented at once. We have his prayer to God in Psalm 51:

> Have mercy on me, O God,
>   according to your unfailing love;
> according to your great compassion
>   blot out my transgressions.
> Wash away all my iniquity
>   and cleanse me from my sin.
>
> For I know my transgressions
>   and my sin is always before me.
> Against you, you only, have I sinned
>   and done what is evil in your sight,
> so that you are proved right when
>   you speak
>   and justified when you judge.
> Surely I have been a sinner from birth,
>   sinful from the time my mother
>   conceived me.

There is no self-righteousness here, no attempt to justify himself. Instead there is a recognition that this sin like every other is an act of rebellion against a good and just God. David feels his defilement,

> Cleanse me with hyssop, and I shall be clean;
>   wash me, and I shall be whiter than snow.
> Hide your face from my sins
>   and blot out all my iniquity.

Above all he wants to come back into the old relationship with the God he loves and trusts.

> Create in me a pure heart, O God,
>   and renew a steadfast spirit within me.
> Do not cast me from your presence
>   or take your Holy Spirit from me.

> Restore to me the joy of your salvation
> and grant me a willing spirit to sustain me.
>
> The sacrifices of God are a broken spirit;
> a broken and contrite heart,
> O God you will not despise.

There can be no doubt of David's repentance and of God's acceptance of it. The son of David's adultery died, but Bathsheba went on to bear him Solomon and from him came the royal line of Judah. Though the kingdom ceased because of Judah's rebellion against God, the promise of the Messiah and the eternal kingdom continued.

This public sin, however, broke David's moral authority, first in his own family and then in the nation. His peak had passed. He reigned on, but in trouble and rebellion. He was reconciled to God, but the human consequences of what he had done continued. There is one last footnote to the story. David was finally persuaded to go and join in the siege of Rabbah. Joab had written to him, 'I have fought against Rabbah and taken its water supply. Now muster the rest of the troops and besiege the city and capture it. Otherwise I shall take the city and it will be named after me.'

So, the chronicler tells us, 'David mustered the entire army and went to Rabbah and attacked and captured it.'

Trouble in the family

God had forgiven David his sin in taking Uriah's wife and then sending Uriah to his death. But the consequences of his deed were to blight the rest of his reign. He lost the respect of his family and could no longer control them. Bathsheba was David's eighth wife, so there was no single mother to influence them.

A look at the list of wives and eldest sons helps to show the divisions in David's family.

1. Michal, daughter of Saul   (no issue)
2. Ahinoam of Jezreel   Amnon
3. Abigail   Kileab

4.	Maacah of Geshur	Absalom
5.	Haggith	Adonijah
6.	Abitail	Shepthatiah
7.	Eglah	Ithream
8.	Bathsheba	Solomon (Jedidiah)

We can well imagine that the natural jealousies between the wives produced jealousies between the families and that it needed a strong ruler, commanding everyone's respect, to keep these natural factions in order. Especially within the family, however, David's actions had lost him all respect and the princes did what they liked.

David was now the most powerful ruler outside Egypt. Foreign princes came to court and also people from the kingdoms David had conquered. Power and influence were to be found in Jerusalem. The leader of simple soldiers became a Middle Eastern potentate, surrounded by the intrigues of those who wielded power and influence, chief of whom were the princes, the king's sons and around them the lesser courtiers full of worldly wisdom.

Amnon's crime

The first prince to get out of hand was the eldest, Amnon. The record tells us that, 'He fell in love with Tamar, the beautiful sister of Absalom.'

There are among courtiers always those who are prepared to ingratiate themselves with the heir-apparent, and his cousin Jonadab suggested a way in which Amnon could be left alone with Tamar. So Amnon pretended to be sick and asked David to send him Tamar to cook him a meal. He then sent everyone else out and asked Tamar to bring what she had baked into his bedroom. She, there on the king's command and trusting her half-brother, brought it in. Amnon grabbed her, raped her and then, having humiliated her, the record tells us, 'Amnon hated her with intense hatred. In fact he hated her more than he had loved her.'

Amnon told her to get out. She protested that this was an even greater wrong than what he had already done, but he sent for his personal servant and told him, 'Get this woman out of here and bolt the door after her.'

What started as moral chaos now developed as an unforgiving hatred between the brothers. Kileab, the son of Abigail, had been the next eldest, but we hear nothing of him. Absalom seems to see himself at this stage as the next in line to Amnon and evidently felt that there was more at stake than his sister's disgrace. He took her in and told her not to take it to heart. David was furious, but who was he to deliver moral lectures to his son? Meantime Absalom let the affair die down. He did not want to take revenge until his half-brother had dropped his guard. Then he could strike suddenly and decisively not only to avenge his sister, but, more importantly, to remove the older son of David who was between him and the succession.

Amnon's murder

Two years later, at sheep-shearing, Absalom asked the king and his officials to join him for the occasion. As no doubt Absalom had calculated, David declined the invitation. Absalom then pressed for Amnon to come instead. Absalom had carefully shown no signs of his hatred of Amnon and though David at first demurred, he seemed to have had a soft spot for Absalom and did eventually send Amnon and 'the rest of the king's sons'.

The scene was set for murder. Absalom told his men that as soon as Amnon was drunk and in high spirits, they were to kill him. Taken by surprise, none of the rest of David's sons were prepared to stand up to Absalom. They all mounted their mules and fled back to Jerusalem. The rumour travelled faster, but reported all David's sons dead. The smooth Jonadab, who had transferred his easy loyalty from Amnon to Absalom, told the king not to worry, that only Amnon was dead. He excused Absalom, saying, 'This has been Absalom's expressed intention ever since the day that Amnon raped his sister Tamar.'

Absalom fled in the other direction, to his uncle, who was the son of the King of Geshur, Absalom's grandfather. Far from condemning Absalom for taking the law into his own hands and murdering his brother, David 'mourned for his son every day'. Where now was the king who respected and upheld God's law? The evident paralysis of will began to be obvious in the court and those around the king must have begun at this point to wonder what could be done about it.

The first to take action was the army commander, Joab. It did the nation no good to have the king wrapped in a paralysis of grief. If David was not going to condemn Absalom, then, thought Joab, he had better have him back and then he could address his mind again to affairs of state. But he didn't tackle David directly on a matter so personal and emotional. Instead he sent for a wise woman from Tekoa and sent her in to the king. She told the king that she was a widow with two sons, one of whom had killed his brother and was now condemned to die, leaving her totally bereft. She ended piteously, 'They would put out the only burning coal I have left, leaving my husband neither name nor descendant on the face of the earth.'

Ignoring the law of Moses, David arbitrarily ruled in her favour. As soon as he had done so, the woman, following Joab's instructions, applied his leniency to the case of his own family. She philosophized, 'Like water spilled on the ground which cannot be recovered, so we must die. But God does not take away life; instead he devises ways in which a banished person may not remain estranged from him.'

This was total casuistry, with no foundation at all in Israel's law, and it was also heavily larded with flattery. The king also recognized that Joab had put her up to it. But, as Joab had hoped, it appealed to him and he told Joab to bring Absalom back, though with orders to keep to his own house and not come to court.

Absalom steals the hearts of the people

This limitation lasted only two years. Absalom not only touched the heart of the king, he touched the heart of the people. He was handsome, was without the slightest flaw and had a great head of hair. He had three sons and a beautiful daughter – and he was ambitious. The ban on his attendance at court not only kept him under a cloud of royal disapproval, it also kept him away from the influential people round the king. He pressed Joab to come to see him. Joab refused. No doubt he could see trouble ahead. After Joab had refused the second time, Absalom, ruthless as ever, sent his servants to burn Joab's standing barley, which was in the next field to his. Then Joab came and Absalom asked him to intercede again with the king. Joab finally agreed. The king saw Absalom and gave him a kiss of reconciliation. Absalom was not only back in Jerusalem, he was now respectable. He could talk to anyone and anyone could talk to him.

Throughout the history of monarchies, the heir-apparent has been the focus of discontent. As reigns go on, so the number of those who have suffered some real or imagined wrong grows inexorably. Democracies deal with the problem by having elections every four or five years. Governments cannot please all of the people all of the time and there comes a point when even a good government has taken too many unpopular decisions and finds that it has exhausted its goodwill. That is the time to call an election and ask for a renewed mandate. But when your ageing hero on the throne is slow to deliver judgment or, worse still, becomes arbitrary in the judgments he does deliver, the climate becomes ripe for the heir-apparent who will promise anything to anyone.

'If only,' said Absalom, sitting at the gate as the litigants came through to the king's court, 'If only I were appointed judge in the land! Then everyone who has a case or complaint could come to me and I would see that he received justice.' He was not only young and handsome, he was approachable; he took them by the hand and kissed them. Absalom had nothing to learn from the modern democratic politician out to woo the voters. 'And so he stole the hearts of the men of Israel.'

5
Rebellion and crisis

Absalom's rebellion

After four years, Absalom was ready to bid for the throne. In six years he had established himself and in those six years David had done nothing, his moral authority paralysed and his self-confidence gone. When, finally, Absalom asked to go to Hebron to fulfil a vow, David let him go, evidently not sensing any danger.

Once in Hebron, Absalom sent messages throughout Israel, calling them to proclaim him king as soon as they got the signal. He also sent for Ahitophel, David's closest counsellor, who came over to his side. When David heard that, he was distraught. It may be then that he wrote,

> Even my close friend, whom I trusted,
>   he who shared my bread,
>   has lifted up his heel against me.
>
> (Psalm 41:9)

Even more eloquently, he wrote,

> If an enemy were insulting me,
>   I could endure it;
> if a foe were raising himself against me,
>   I could hide from him.
> But it is you, a man like myself,
>   my companion, my close friend,
> with whom I once enjoyed sweet fellowship
>   as we walked with the throng at
>   the house of God.
>
> (Psalm 55:12)

But whatever he felt, the old warrior knew how to act. He may not have been much good in a musty lawcourt, but his son had taken up arms against the best general in the ancient world. David felt unsafe in Jerusalem. Absalom had had time to raise an army and if he had stayed in the capital he would be a sitting duck. He had to get out into the country as soon as he could to raise his own army. He had to head beyond the Jordan, where he could not be surprised and where he was still a hero to those whom he had recently delivered from the Ammonite threat.

Despite the circumstances of Uriah's death, the army was loyal. They were not going to exchange their veteran leader for an untried young prince with long hair and charming manners. The standing army and the guards' regiments marched with the king together with government officials and the priests carrying the ark. But David needed information about what was going on in Jerusalem and he sent back the priests, Zadok and Abiathar, with their sons. He instructed them to keep him informed. He also sent back Hushai the Arkite, a valued adviser, telling him to declare loyalty to Absalom and to try to counter the advice of Ahitophel.

When Absalom arrived in Jerusalem, he asked both Ahitophel and Hushai to advise him. Ahitophel gave him what was undoubtedly the correct advice, to follow David as fast as he could and to defeat him before he could recover from his flight, organize himself and raise his own army. He also advised him to kill only David, so that he did not alienate anyone else and could therefore reunite the people as fast as possible.

Then Absalom asked Hushai, who, to protect David, gave the opposite advice. He said that the cornered army was experienced and desperate, and would fight like a bear robbed of its whelps. Such was their reputation that, on the slightest setback, the rumours would spread that Absalom's force had been defeated. As for killing David only, his army would hide him where no-one could find him. On the contrary, said Hushai, Absalom should raise an army so large that there would be nowhere for David and his troops to hide.

Absalom, playing as he thought for safety, followed Hushai's advice and decided not to strike at once. In his vanity he fatally overestimated his own popularity and underestimated his father's legendary reputation. He did not realize that he had lost the momentum needed to rush David while he was weak and had given David and Joab's veterans the vital time needed to rally a matching army around skilled and tried commanders.

Hushai sent a message immediately by Jonathan and Ahimaaz, the sons of the two priests, who left at once to tell David and Joab that they had time to raise an army to fight Absalom. They were seen, but after being hidden down a well, they escaped and got through to David to tell him what had happened and to give Hushai's advice that he should keep moving east beyond Jordan. By daybreak David and all the people with him were over the river.

When Ahitophel saw that his advice had not been taken, he knew that Absalom's cause was hopeless. He went home, put his affairs in order and hanged himself, the first casualty of the rebellion.

Across the river, in the border country of Gilead, David was in a strategic position to gather support from both Judah and Israel. David took up his quarters in Mahanaim and there he found friendly hands who provisioned his army. Absalom appointed Amasa, cousin to both Joab and David, as his army commander and eventually they followed David across the Jordan.

On Absalom's approach David divided his army into three and put in charge of each division one of the veteran leaders who had fought in all his great battles, Joab, Abishai his brother and Ittai, the Gittite. He wanted to go with them, but they would not let him. He was Absalom's target and if he were killed all would be lost. 'Even if half of us die, they won't care, but you are worth ten thousand of us.'

We are told that the battle took place in 'the forest of Ephraim'. We must suppose that David's commanders used their three separate forces to manoeuvre Amasa into the wooded country where he could not deploy superior numbers and where the experienced veterans could attack and demolish them piecemeal. Absalom's army lost twenty thousand and we are told, 'the forest claimed more lives that day than the sword'.

Absalom's death

One of those trapped in the forest was Absalom, whose long hair had got caught up in an oak while his mule went on, leaving him hanging. One of David's men found him and told Joab. Joab asked why he had not killed him at once and the soldier replied that it was more than his life was worth because the king had ordered the three commanders, 'Protect the young man Absalom for my sake.'

Joab had no time for sentiment. Absalom would have had none. If there was to be peace in Israel, it was David's life or Absalom's. He struck his javelin through Absalom's heart and ten of his men finished him off. Then Joab sounded the cease-fire. Once Absalom had gone, no-one else need die. Ruthless though Joab was, he had a rough logic which his soldiers would understand. Thousands had died in a great battle for this one man's ambition and Joab wanted no more to die.

David, however, did not see Absalom's death like that. When he heard the news, he went to his room and wept. 'Oh, my son Absalom! My son, my son Absalom! If only I had died instead of you – Oh Absalom my son, my son!'

No doubt David felt a responsibility for the faulty upbringing of a son who had gone astray, guilty that his own adultery had fatally undermined his moral authority and had set off the whole sorry process which had led to Absalom's death. But when Joab was told, he was furious. The victorious army who had risked their lives and had saved the kingdom were creeping into the city as if they had just been defeated.

Joab went to see David and said, 'Today you have humiliated all your men who have just saved your life and the lives of your sons and daughters and the lives of your wives and concubines. You love those who hate you and hate those who love you. You have made it clear that the commanders and their men mean nothing to you. I see that you would be pleased if Absalom were alive today and all of us were dead. Now go out and encourage your men. I swear by the Lord that if you don't go out, not a man will be left with you by nightfall.'

David had to listen to Joab. He pulled himself together and

went down to the gate and all the men gathered round the king whose throne they had just saved.

David's return to Jerusalem

The northern tribes now felt very guilty about David, remembering all he had done for them and it looked as though they would be the first to ask him back. So David sent a message to the priests, suggesting that his own tribe of Judah should not be left behind. 'You are my brothers, my own flesh and blood, so why should you be the last to bring back the king?' So Judah came out to welcome David back to Jerusalem but the volatile northern tribes were turned against him by a trouble-maker called Sheba.

In addition, in the same kind of gesture of reconciliation that he had made to Saul's commander Abner, he appointed Amasa, Absalom's commander, to be commander of his forces in place of Joab. Fatally for Amasa, however, Joab responded to the gesture as he had responded to the appointment of Abner. David asked Amasa to summon troops from Judah to deal with Sheba and his rebellious following among the northern tribes. This must have been an impossible task for someone who had just been leading a rebellion himself and Judah does not seem to have responded with any speed. So David decided that faster action was needed. He turned to Abishai, who led the guards, veterans and Joab's men out against Sheba before he could find shelter in a fortified city.

Amasa met them. Joab greeted him, made as if to kiss him and killed him with one blow of his dagger. Joab at once took command again and everyone followed him. They went unopposed through Israel until they came to the city where Sheba had taken refuge. Such was Joab's reputation that the city, rather than face Joab, executed Sheba and threw his head over the wall. So the rebellion finally ended, the country was reunited and Joab retained his command and his ascendancy. But David did not forgive or forget Amasa's murder.

Like any disaster, the rebellion of Absalom had a number of causes, none of which by itself would have been enough to tip the country into catastrophe.

Absalom's mother was not only a foreigner to Israel. She came from the royal line of Geshur, a corrupt country which, with the adjoining country of the Philistines, Joshua had been told to conquer. Up to Saul's time they had remained hostile neighbours, their religious practices far removed from those of Israel. So it is most unlikely that Absalom's mother had brought him up with any respect for the God of Israel or for the law of Moses. When Absalom murdered his half-brother Amnon, he had fled for asylum to his royal relations in Geshur. He must have known that they would receive him and that says a good deal about where his natural sympathies lay. Absalom did not have his father's love for Jehovah or any part of his faith. Opposing his father came naturally.

All this might have been put right had David had only one wife. Then the father would have been as much to the son as the mother. But David had at least eight wives, eight rival families and the mother was the one who fought for her child against the others, the one to whom the child's loyalty naturally went. David's great faith might communicate itself to the nation, but not to the son of his Geshurite wife.

Despite all this, David might have commanded the respect of his family and had their obedience. But his adultery with Uriah's wife and the way in which he sent Uriah to his death, removed all his moral authority as a father. He had repented most bitterly and God had forgiven him, but the family did not forget. Faced with Amnon's rape, he took no action. Faced with Absalom's murder of Amnon, he allowed his son back from exile and eventually received him at court. Absalom exploited a moral vacuum.

David might still have been able to contain Absalom's ambition had he kept the hearts of the people. This may have been something to do with a continuing sense of shame on his part, a corresponding feeling on the part of the people that their former idol had feet of clay. But though he had, as the psalms show, a strong sense of justice, it also seems to have been hard for him to make the transition from the soldier king to the king at peace, the lawgiver who not only cares for the wrongs of the poor and weak, but can be relied on to see that justice is done through the long and wearisome hearing of legal arguments. This is the weakness which Absalom actually exploited, the role which Solomon filled so brilliantly.

Whatever had gone wrong, David knew who had put it right.

> He is the God who avenges me,
>   who puts the nations under me,
>   who sets me free from my
>   enemies.
> You exalted me above my foes,
>   from violent men you rescued me.
> Therefore I will praise you, O LORD
>   among the nations;
>   I will sing praises to your name.
>   (2 Samuel 22:48–50)

The Philistines' last attack

There was one final rebellion against David. It came from Israel's old enemies, the Philistines. For one last time David went out to battle and had it not been for a swift rescue by Abishai, an exhausted David would have been killed.

David's men decided that he had fought his last battle. They said, 'Never again will you go out to battle, so that the light of Israel will not be extinguished.'

The Philistines came back two further times and after that we hear no more about them. David's kingdom was complete, ready for Israel's golden age. His faith in God was justified. Small though Israel was, it had, under David, been delivered from all the enemies which had surrounded it since its arrival in the land hundreds of years before. David acknowledged this in a great song of praise.

> The LORD is my rock, my fortress
>   and my deliverer;
>   my God is my rock, in whom I
>   take refuge.
> He is my shield and the horn of

my salvation, my stronghold.
I call to the LORD, who is worthy of praise
    and I am saved from my enemies.

He reached down from on high
    and took hold of me;
    he drew me out of deep waters.
He rescued me from my powerful enemy,
    from the foes who were too strong for me.
They confronted me in the day of
        my disaster,
    but the LORD was my support.

With your help I can advance
    against a troop;
    with my God I can scale a wall.

He makes my feet like the feet of a deer;
    he enables me to stand on the heights.
He trains my hands for battle;
    my arms can bend a bow of bronze.

You armed me with strength for battle;
    you made my adversaries bow at my feet.

You have delivered me from the
        attacks of the people;
    you have made me the head of
        nations;
    people I did not know are subject to me.
As soon as they hear me, they obey me;
    foreigners cringe before me.
They all lose heart;
    they come trembling from their strongholds.

He is the God who avenges me,
    who subdues nations under me,
    who saves me from my enemies.

You exalted me above my foes;
   from violent men you rescued me.
Therefore I will praise you among
   the nations, O LORD;
   I will sing praises to your name.
He gives his king great victories;
   he shows unfailing kindness to
     his anointed,
    to David and his descendants for ever.

(Psalm 18)

David's last failure

After the last rebellion had been defeated, David's faith unaccountably failed.

The king had never depended on expensive horses and chariots, had always relied on a voluntary citizens' call to arms and trusted in God to supply all his needs. Suddenly he became like any other eastern despot and called for a registering of manpower throughout Israel. This enabled him to calculate the strength of a conscript army against the other powers around his wider borders; the Hittites in the north and the Egyptians in the south.

Before Samuel anointed Saul, he had warned Israel that if they chose a monarchy, this is what a king would do. He said, 'He will take your sons and make them serve with his chariots and horses, and they will run in front of his chariots . . . and you yourselves will become his slaves' (1 Samuel 8:11, 17).

It was Samuel who had anointed David too, so David must have had this warning from Samuel himself, even if he had missed the great gathering before Saul was made king. Even Joab, the hardened army chief, knew that David's order was wrong and protested against it. 'May the LORD your God multiply your troops a hundred times over, and may the eye of my lord the king see it. But why does my lord the king want to do such a thing?'

The army commanders supported Joab, but David insisted and they went out to enrol the fighting men of Israel.

It took nearly ten months and the tally was impressive, eight hundred thousand able-bodied swordsmen in the northern tribes and five hundred thousand in Judah.

At heart David was still a man of faith, however, and when they came back he was conscience-stricken at what he had done. Now that he had enrolled Israel he had to face the question which he had not faced before – what was he going to do with this military strength? Was he, like any other despot, going to go out to fight without asking God? If anyone attacked Israel, was he going to rely on his great numbers instead of relying on God? He remembered all his enemies who had relied on their great strength and whom he had defeated only with God's help.

David turned to God and said, 'I have sinned greatly in what I have done. Now, O LORD, I beg you, take away the guilt of your servant. I have done a very foolish thing.'

David had not been alone in his imperial arrogance and in forgetfulness of the God who had honoured his faith, the God whom everyone had acknowledged as the giver of all their victories. The whole people had been carried away by their new power and prosperity and had aroused God's anger. David, who should have rebuked their new mood, instead gave it expression.

Gad the prophet gave David three options from the Lord. David could choose three years of famine, three months of flight before his enemies or three days of plague. David chose the plague. 'Let us fall into the hands of God, for his mercies are great but do not let me fall into the hands of men.'

David was right about God's mercy. Seventy thousand died in the plague. Then David said to the Lord, 'I am the one who has sinned and done wrong. These are but sheep. What have they done. Let your hand fall on me and my family.'

God, however, halted the plague on the outskirts of Jerusalem at the threshing-floor of Araunah the Jebusite.

The Lord told David to build an altar there, so he bought the threshing-floor from Araunah, built his altar and sacrificed on the place where his son Solomon was to build Israel's permanent altar and the great temple around it.

Adonijah's bid for the succession

David had one more crisis to surmount. He was ageing and, not surprisingly, the circle around him began to look to the succession. Amnon, his oldest son, was dead and so was Absalom. Adonijah, son of Haggith, David's fifth wife, considered himself next in line and secured the support of Joab the army commander, and of Abiathar the priest. Joab may have felt that Adonijah would be more pliable than the formidable Solomon, who was David's choice. The moment was ripe for a *coup d'état*.

But Zadok the other priest did not support Abiathar, however, nor did Nathan the prophet, Beniah the son of Jehoida, the royal counsellor, or the royal guard.

David had promised Bathsheba that the succession would go to their son Solomon. He evidently saw in this much younger son all the promise of the wisdom which was later to emerge. He had done nothing, however, about this decision. David, like many a ruler reluctant finally to concede power, may have delayed the announcement of his successor. He may also have been preoccupied with the plans for the great temple; or, cared for by Abishag, his new wife and companion, who was young and beautiful, he may have been cut off from the sharp ears and eyes which could have kept him in touch.

With David old, and evidently out of touch, and no official announcement of a successor, Adonijah decided that the moment had come to seize power. So he invited all his half-brothers, except Solomon, to a feast, together with the royal officials, except for those he knew to be loyal to David. The purpose of the feast was to announce himself as king and to secure their endorsement there and then.

Nathan and Bathsheba appeal to the king

Nathan saw that he had to act at once. The king had made a promise to Bathsheba, so Nathan sent Bathsheba to the king first, to remind him of his promise and to tell him that Adonijah had declared himself king without David's knowledge. She said to David that it was for him to decide who was to succeed him. 'My lord the king the eyes of all Israel are on you to learn from you who will sit on the throne of my lord the king after him.'

She pointed out that otherwise, as soon as David died, she and their son Solomon would be treated as criminals. Nathan, as arranged, followed Bathsheba with the same story and asked whether the king had authorized Adonijah's succession without telling his senior advisers.

David appoints Solomon king

David, in this last crisis, became once more the man of action. He called Bathsheba back and swore again, 'By the Lord God of Israel, Solomon your son shall be king after me and he will sit on my throne in my place.' Then he called for Zadok the priest, Nathan the prophet and Benaiah his counsellor, told them to put Solomon on the king's mule and then to set him on David's throne to reign in his place. David, having judged the remarkable quality of Solomon, must have reckoned that the people would have come to the same judgment and would endorse his choice with enthusiasm. He was right: 'And all the people shouted "Long live King Solomon!" And all the people went up with him, playing flutes and rejoicing greatly, so that the ground shook with the sound.' No conspiracy could stand against that.

Abiathar's son Jonathan reported to the conspirators, 'Zadok the priest and Nathan the prophet have anointed (Solomon) king at Gihon. From there they have gone up cheering, and the city resounds with it. That's the noise you hear.'

The conspirators melted away and Adonijah submitted to Solomon, who warned him to be on good behaviour.

Solomon establishes his throne

David's first advice to Solomon was to walk in God's ways and to keep his commands. But he also had unfinished business. The most important was the two unpunished murders of Joab. David said to Solomon, 'You yourself know . . . what he did to the two commanders of Israel's armies, Abner son of Ner and Amasa son of Jether. He killed them, shedding their blood in peacetime as if in battle . . . Deal with him according to your wisdom, but do not let his grey head go down to the grave in peace.'

David's intentions were clear. He left it to Solomon to find a way of carrying them out.

Solomon may have had the people's cheers, his father's blessing, the support of most of his chief advisers and his Royal Guard. But when David died, he still had against him a very frustrated older brother and the formidable and legendary commander of the army, who had not hesitated to kill his relative Amasa against the king's express order. Solomon's older brother showed his hand first. After David's death Adonijah came to see Bathsheba, still burning with resentment. 'As you know, the kingdom was mine. All Israel looked to me as their king. But things changed.'

It was clear from this that he believed that he had not only the right of age, but of popular support and that he had conceded nothing of his claim. Then he asked Bathsheba to ask Solomon to give him David's beautiful young widow, Abishag, as his wife.

Solomon treated the request for King David's widow as a first step in a claim to the throne and said to his mother, 'You might as well request the kingdom for him – after all, he is my older brother – yes, for him and for Abiathar the priest and Joab son of Zeruiah.'

Behind Adonijah was the looming figure of the ruthless army commander, to whom assassination was second nature. Behind Joab was a battle-hardened army, many of whose leaders – including Joab's brother – would have more loyalty to their trusted commander than to the stripling Solomon, installed, as they would be told, by a senile king under pressure from an ambitious mother. No doubt there would be some who would remember David's treatment of Bathsheba's first husband, who had held the army's highest honours.

So Adonijah's boldness was a danger signal to Solomon. As David saw Joab's hand in the request for Absalom's return to Jerusalem, so Solomon must have seen Joab's hand in Adonijah's request for King David's young widow. Solomon did not wait for open rebellion, he struck at once. He had given Adonijah a warning which he had not respected, so he ordered his immediate execution.

With his candidate dead, Joab's scheme was finished. He had met his match and he knew it. He fled to the sanctuary of the tabernacle and seized the horns of the altar. Solomon, remembering his father's words about Joab's unpunished murders, ordered him to be executed where he was. Abiathar he removed from the priesthood and ordered back to his village. Solomon had secured his kingdom.

Solomon's temple

Before David died, he had called together Solomon and all his officials. David had been making all the preparations for the great temple which Solomon would build and he wanted to hand the work over.

1 Chronicles 18:11, 13 tells us, 'David gave his son Solomon the plans for the portico of the temple, its buildings, its storerooms, its upper parts, its inner rooms and the place of atonement . . . as well as for all the articles to be used in its service.'

'All this is in writing,' David said, 'because the hand of the LORD was upon me, and he gave me understanding in all the details of the plan . . . With all my resources I have provided for the temple of my God – gold for the gold work, silver for the silver . . . I now give my personal treasures of gold and silver for the temple of my God: three thousand talents of gold . . . Now, who is willing to consecrate himself today to the LORD?'

'Then the leaders of the families, the officers of the tribes of Israel, the commanders . . . the officials . . . gave willingly . . . five thousand talents of gold . . . The people rejoiced at the willing response of their leaders, for they had given freely and wholeheartedly to the Lord. David the king also rejoiced greatly.'

God did not want David, a man of blood, to build the temple. Solomon built it and it has always been known as Solomon's temple. But David was the architect; he raised the money, organized the priests, the Levites and the singers and, as his last act, gained the public commitment of all those who led his country to the creation of this centre of worship to glorify the God he loved and trusted.

Then he led them in a final prayer which expresses his love for God and his total faith in his goodness.

> Praise be to you, O LORD
>   God of our father Israel,
>   from everlasting to everlasting.
> Yours, O LORD, is the greatness and
>   the power
>   and the glory and the majesty
>   and the splendour,
>   for everything in heaven and
>   earth is yours.
> Yours, O LORD, is the kingdom;
>   you are exalted as head over all.
> Wealth and honour come from you;
>   you are the ruler of all things.
> In your hands are strength and power
>   to exalt and give strength to all.
> Now, our God, we give you thanks
>   and praise your glorious name.

But who am I, and who are my people, that we should be able to give as generously as this? Everything comes from you, and we have given you only what comes from your hand. We are aliens and strangers in your sight, as were all our forefathers. Our days on earth are like a shadow, without hope. O LORD our God, as for all this abundance that we have provided for building you a temple for your Holy Name, it comes from your hand, and all of it belongs to you. I know, my God, that you test the heart and are pleased with integrity. All these things have I given willingly and with honest intent. And now I have seen with joy how willingly your people who are here have given to you.

O LORD, God of our fathers Abraham, Isaac and Israel, keep this desire in the hearts of your people for ever, and keep their hearts loyal to you. And give my son Solomon the wholehearted devotion to keep your commands, requirements and decrees to do everything to build the palatial structure for which I have provided.

David had organized the singers in Jerusalem so that they would be ready for the great temple which he had planned. 'David set apart some of the sons of Asaph, Heman and Jeduthun for the ministry of prophesying, accompanied by harps, lyres and cymbals. The six sons of Jeduthun prophesied, using the harp in thanksgiving and praising God.' The sons of all three fathers and their relations – nearly three hundred – were 'all of them trained and skilled in music for the Lord'.

With the king's personal interest, it must have been a remarkable choir and orchestra!

This was not music for music's sake or art for art's sake. David was a prophet, with a vision of God which he wanted to share with all the people. And the God who gave him the vision also gave him the gifts needed to pass it on. That combination of vision and art is the genius of David's poetry. Even today, it is to David we go when we want to put our feelings about God in the most expressive words.

It must have comforted David at the end of a life in which he had made many mistakes that he was leaving the plans for this great house of God, the singers and players to remind future generations of the greatness of the God he had known so well and loved so much.

Part 2

David our contemporary

6

'A man after God's own heart'

The personality of David shines through his story. He is brave, loyal, warm-hearted and generous, with a strong sense of justice and a real case for the underdog. But he had, as we have seen, many faults too.

Yet God, after rejecting King Saul, chose David as 'a man after my own heart', to be King of Israel. Not only that, but he promised him that his dynasty would be established and that in the distant future there would be a king from his own line, the Messiah, who would reign for ever. Not since their founding-father Israel, had there been such promises to an individual, and never have there been such promises since.

It is only as we weave together David's deeds with his words that we can see the motives which drove and guided him, the high standards he set himself and the bitter regret which he suffered when he failed to live up to those standards. None of us is perfect, but some set a higher standard for themselves than others and some see and correct their failures instead of ignoring or excusing them. Whatever David's failures, he set himself what he believed to be the standards of God his Creator, and he felt every failure deeply as an inexcusable and personal offence against the God of Israel who loved him, cared for him and protected him.

David's attitude to God is the key to his whole character.

God's creation

David stood in awe of God. The God of Israel was wholly different from the man-made idols of Israel's neighbours, carved by a village craftsman out of a log and whose left-over chippings were used to light a fire. The first book of Moses taught that there is only one God, the one who has made the visible universe and each person in it and who has given them the Maker's instructions, telling them how to relate to the rest of God's creation and to each other. David believed that we could not create gods, because the one true God had created us. We were not wiser or more far-sighted than our Creator and could no more alter the moral framework he had laid down than we could move the mountains into the sea. David believed that we had only to look at the natural world to see this:

> The heavens declare the glory of God;
>   the skies proclaim the work of his hands.
> Day after day they pour forth speech;
>   night after night they display knowledge.
> There is no speech or language
>   where their voice is not heard.
> Their voice goes out into all the earth,
>   their words to the end of the world.
>
> In the heavens he has pitched a tent
>   for the sun,
>   which is like a bridegroom
>   coming forth from his pavilion,
>   like a champion rejoicing to run his course.
> It rises at one end of the heavens
>   and make its circuit to the other;
>   nothing is hidden from its heat.
>
>   (Psalm 19:1–6)

The first book of Moses taught that God was one God and that there were no others, that he was a God of order and a God of reason. It taught that he was a God who would keep his promise that

> As long as the earth endures,
> seedtime and harvest,
> cold and heat,
> summer and winter,
> day and night
> will never cease.
>
>   (Genesis 8:22)

110

And it taught that he had made the natural world for human benefit. 'Then God said, "I give you every seed-bearing plant on the face of the whole earth and every tree that has fruit with seed in it. They will be yours for food" ' (Genesis 1:29).

So David believed that in the natural order, reflecting the character of the Creator, there was unity, order, reason and stability and that it was benign; qualities we now know as the presuppositions on which modern science was founded. The pagan religions of David's day saw in nature disunity, disorder, irrationality, instability and they believed that, like their gods, nature was malign. That view is not too far from the view of today's new pagans who are returning to the old superstitions from which our world was rescued by the teaching which we inherited from David and others with his faith.

David did not have the scientific knowledge of the details of the Creator's design in the life-systems of the human and animal body or of the eco-systems of plant and animal habitat. But he and everyone else could see God's order there. They could also see the majestic order in the skies above, the absolute regularity of day and night, the waning and waxing of the moon, the regular passage of the stars. David believed that everyone should see them and should recognize the glory of the God who made them. A God who had done that was no mean painted stick of wood. David worshipped an altogether greater God, a God of a totally different order to those dreamed up by a limited human imagination.

In relation to the grandeur and glory of God the Creator, we were nothing; yet God has recognized us and given us the key place as custodians of his creation.

> When I consider your heavens,
>   the work of your fingers,
> the moon and the stars
>   which you have set in place,
> what is man that you are mindful
>   of him,
>   the son of man that you care for him?

111

You made him a little lower than
    the heavenly beings
and crowned him with glory and
    honour.

You made him ruler over the works
    of your hands,
    you put everything under his feet;
all flocks and herds,
    and the beasts of the field,
the birds of the air,
    and the fish of the sea,
    all that swim the paths of the seas.

O LORD, our Lord,
    how majestic is your name in all
      the earth.

                    (Psalm 8:3–9)

Despite all this there were those in David's day, as in ours, who still doubted whether there really was a God. David had little time for them, 'The fool says in his heart "There is no God" ' (Psalm 14:1).

God's law

Everyone could see God's creation and everyone should stand in awe. To Israel, however, God had entrusted the Maker's instructions in written form. The law was given by God to Moses on Mount Sinai with dramatic and unforgettable signs and wonders. Moses had also written an account of all these which was to be passed down faithfully, with the law, from generation to generation. In the same psalm, David moved from God's creation to his law.

The law of the LORD is perfect,
    reviving the soul.
The statutes of the LORD are trustworthy,
    making wise the simple.

The precepts of the LORD are right,
    giving joy to the heart.
The commands of the LORD are radiant,
    giving light to the eyes.
The fear of the LORD is pure,
    enduring for ever.
The ordinances of the LORD are sure
    and altogether righteous.
They are more precious than gold,
    than much pure gold;
They are sweeter than honey,
    than honey from the comb.
By them is your servant warned;
    in keeping them there is great reward.
                     (Psalm 19:7–11)

David's reign came not long after a period of moral chaos in Israel in which 'Israel had no king and everyone did as he saw fit' (Judges 21:25). The result was sodomy, rape, murder, civil war and massacre. Samuel, the last of the judges, had begun again to set the standards of God's law, but, as we have seen, King Saul had increasingly disregarded Samuel's guidance. He had murdered the high priest and, before his last battle, had been reduced to consulting a witch. It needed the combination of David's own deep conviction and his great authority to establish in Israel a true respect for God's law.

David did not see the law as a tool to be used by rulers to keep order among the people. He believed that the law was wise, good and just, that it was there to protect the defenceless from the rich and powerful and that he, as king, was as much under the law of the Lord as the poorest of the people. When he realized that he had broken the law, he was bitterly repentant. When he had committed adultery with Bathsheba and had sent Uriah, her husband, to his death, he realized the enormity of his sin against them both but in his confession he said it was against the Lord above all that he had sinned. He had received so much power and responsibility from the Lord. He had been entrusted with the moral leadership of Israel and he was overcome by the thought that this terrible example was the return he had given to the Lord.

God's justice

There was no question in David's mind that, since God's law was just, he was entitled to punish those who broke it. The king executed justice on God's behalf and, since the king was also under the law, God executed justice on the king. David had waited for God's justice against Saul, refusing to take the law into his own hands. He accepted fully God's right to punish him when he himself broke God's law.

David did not believe that God's law and his justice were confined to Israel. His own great-grandmother, Ruth, had left her native Moab and its gods to come to Israel to serve the true God. His more distant ancestor Rahab, the Canaanite of Jericho, had made the same decision.

Israel's belief in one God was not hidden from all the people round about. Nature itself spoke of a Creator who could not be reduced to a piece of painted wood. So those who, like Rahab and Ruth and many of his own outlaw band, had left their gods for the God of Israel, would be blessed, but the sins of wicked nations would be punished.

> You have rebuked the nations and
>   destroyed the wicked;
>   you have blotted out their name
>   for ever and ever.
> Endless ruin has overtaken the enemy,
>   you have uprooted their cities,
>   even the memory of them has perished.
>
> The LORD reigns for ever;
>   he has established his throne for judgment.
> He will judge the world in righteousness,
>   he will govern the peoples with justice.
> The LORD is a refuge for the oppressed,
>   a stronghold in times of trouble.
>
>   (Psalm 9:5–9)

Here David is thinking of the oppression of Israel by those nations encircling her who sent out raiding-parties at harvest time across Israel's long straggling frontier and who, like the Philistines, attacked her without cause to impose their rule, extort tribute and subvert the true religion.

Most of his pleas against the wicked and evildoers are nearer home, however.

> Help, LORD, for the godly are no more;
>   the faithful have vanished from among men.
> Everyone lies to his neighbour;
>   their flattering lips speak with deception.
>
> May the LORD cut off all flattering lips
>   and every boastful tongue
> that says, 'We will triumph with our tongues;
>   we own our lips – who is our master?'
>
> 'Because of the oppression of the weak
>   and the groaning of the needy,
> I will now arise,' says the LORD.
>   'I will protect them from those who
>   malign them.'
> And the words of the LORD are flawless,
>   like silver refined in a furnace of clay,
>   purified seven times.
>
> O LORD, you will keep us safe
>   and protect us from such people for ever.
> The wicked freely strut about
>   when what is vile is honoured
>   among men.
>
>   (Psalm 12)

He condemns exploitation,

> Will the evildoers never learn –
>   those who devour my people as

> men eat bread
> and who do not call on God?
> (Psalm 53:4)

and attacks on the innocent,

> from that noisy crowd of evildoers,
> who sharpen their tongues like swords
> and aim their words like deadly arrows.
> They shoot from ambush at the innocent man;
> they shoot at him suddenly without fear.
> (Psalm 64:2b–4)

Nearer home, too, in the court itself, there was treachery against God's anointed king, the treachery of Absalom his own son and of Ahitophel his friend and counsellor.

> If an enemy were insulting me,
> I could endure it;
> if a foe were raising himself against me,
> I could hide from him.
> But it is you, a man like myself,
> my companion, my close friend,
> with whom I once enjoyed sweet fellowship
> as we walked with the throng at the house of God.
> (Psalm 55:12–14)

> His speech is smooth as butter,
> yet war is in his heart;
> his words are more soothing than oil,
> yet they are drawn swords.
> (Psalm 55:21)

Even here, David trusts in God's justice.

> Cast your cares on the LORD
> and he will sustain you;
> he will never let the righteous fall.

116

But you, O God, will bring down
   the wicked
  into the pit of corruption;
bloodthirsty and deceitful men
   will not live out half their days.

But as for me, I trust in you.
          (Psalm 55:22–23)

Today, with the abolition in so many countries of capital punishment, the justice dispensed by David may seem bloodthirsty. But in executing murderers, David was keeping to the law. The first book of Moses recorded the covenant by which God promised stability of the natural laws and protection of mankind against universal catastrophe. One of the two conditions for this covenant was capital punishment for murder.

Whoever sheds the blood of man,
   by man shall his blood be shed;
for in the image of God
   has God made man.
          (Genesis 9:6)

Our generation says that to inflict capital punishment for murder degrades the dignity of the human being. David's God said that those who dared to take the life of a person made in his own image no longer had the right to live among human beings. We who live in an age of unprecedented murder and violence should hesitate before deciding that we are right and that Israel's laws are wrong.

God's forgiveness to all who ask for his mercy

David's God was just, but he listened to the penitent, and with judgment also came mercy and forgiveness.

Remember not the sins of my youth
   and my rebellious ways;

> according to your love remember me,
>> for you are good, O LORD.
>>> (Psalm 25:7)

> For the sake of your name, O LORD,
>> forgive my iniquity, though it is great.
>>> (Psalm 25:11)

> O LORD, do not rebuke me in your anger
>> or discipline me in your wrath.
> For your arrows have pierced me,
>> and your hand has come down upon me.
> Because of your wrath there is no health
>> in my body;
>> my bones have no soundness because of my sin.
> My guilt has overwhelmed me
>> like a burden too heavy to bear.
>>> (Psalm 38:1–4)

In addition we have David's agonized confessions (quoted in chapter 4) when Nathan brought home to him the enormity of his guilt in taking Uriah's wife and in sending Uriah to his death. That sin brought its own punishment, but God's acceptance of David's confession was shown in his gift of David's chosen successor, the great Solomon, born to David by Bathsheba.

The law of Moses prescribed sacrifices to atone for sins, but David as a prophet talks of God himself atoning for sin.

> O you who hear prayer,
>> to you all men will come.
> When we were overwhelmed by sins,
>> you atoned for our transgressions.
>>> (Psalm 65:2–3)

> You answer us with awesome deeds
>> of righteousness,
> O God our Saviour,

118

> the hope of all the ends of the earth
> and of the farthest seas.
>
> (Psalm 65:5)

David himself gives only the faintest outline of the Saviour who will descend from his line. This faint outline is sharpened by the great prophets in the centuries following and that is the subject of the next chapter on 'Great David's greater Son'.

God's love, protection and guidance

If there is any one point of David's character which, above all the others, makes him a man after God's own heart, it is his implicit faith and trust in God. His faith that God was with him enabled him to fight Goliath. There may have been many who had David's skill with the sling, but none had the faith to take on the giant in single combat. It was his faith, that the God who had sent Samuel to anoint him would surely bring him to the throne, which kept him through his years as an outlaw. It was faith in God which prevented him twice, when it was in his power, from killing Saul. Whenever he wanted to know whether to go up to battle, he asked the Lord and when God told him to go, he went. When, in Absalom's rebellion, all seemed against him, he still trusted God. We know all this because he has told us.

> I will lie down and sleep in peace,
> for you alone, O LORD,
> make me dwell in safety.
>
> (Psalm 4:8)

> I trust in your unfailing love.
> (Psalm 13:5a)

> Some trust in chariots and some in horses,
> but we trust in the name of the
> LORD our God.
>
> (Psalm 20:7)

> The LORD is my shepherd, I shall
> lack nothing.
>
> (Psalm 23:1)

> They conspire against me
> and plot to take my life.
> But I trust in you, O LORD;
> I say, 'You are my God.'
>
> (Psalm 31:13b–14)

> From the ends of the earth, I call to you,
> I call as my heart grows faint;
> lead me to the rock that is higher
> than I.
>
> (Psalm 61:2)

> My soul finds rest in God alone;
> my salvation comes from him.
> He alone is my rock and my salvation;
> he is my fortress, I shall never be shaken.
>
> (Psalm 62:1–2)

Patience

Because David trusted in God, he was not in a hurry; he was content to wait for God's time. He was not in a hurry to marry one of Saul's daughters. He was content to leave his fellow officers and, as a humble harpist, go back to court to soothe Saul's nerves. He waited during the long years in the wilderness until it was God's time to bring him to the kingdom. He was content to wait for seven years in Hebron as king of Judah until the other clans were ready to call him to rule over them too. He accepted that he was not the person to build the great temple, that this had to wait until Solomon's time. But he used the time in preparing the designs of the temple and its contents. He was in a hurry when God wanted him to be in a hurry, but was happy to wait when God wanted him to wait.

Wait for the LORD;
be strong and take heart
and wait for the LORD.
(Psalm 27:14)

Be still before the LORD and wait
patiently for him;
do not fret when men succeed in
their ways,
when they carry out their wicked
schemes.

Refrain from anger and turn from wrath;
do not fret – it leads only to evil.
For evil men will be cut off
but those who hope in the LORD
will inherit the land.
(Psalm 37:7–9)

I have seen a wicked and ruthless man
flourishing like a green tree in its native soil,
but he soon passed away and was
no more;
though I looked for him, he could
not be found.
(Psalm 37:35–36)

Worship

We live in an age which is almost totally lacking in any sense of awe. All the veils have been ripped away. The camera goes from the highest mountains to the deepest oceans, the famous are over-exposed on TV and then ruthlessly ignored and forgotten. We know too much and too little. We have skimmed the surface of so much that we think that the tight TV 30-minute package has explored everything and have no idea of the depth of our own ignorance.

Our travel is packaged too. As the guides take us round the

great cathedrals, we find out when they were built and in what style, who was buried there and who was crowned, but we are told nothing of the inspiration to worship which compelled people with a fraction of our income to erect to the glory of God a building where cost was no object. Only a tiny number of cathedral visitors today stay to worship.

No doubt the medieval cathedrals were too extravagant and the methods of funding them oppressive, but the Middle Ages did have a sense of awe and worship which our generation has lost.

We, of course, have our idols of screen, song and sport. But we like to be able to throw them over when we are tired of them. Furthermore, it is socially acceptable to be devoted to some trivial pursuit, to be mad on opera or pigeons, riding or cycling, vintage cars or jazz, because it is our own choice and it has no claim on us or on our friends.

We are so steeped in our secular, materialistic, humanist society that the idea of worshipping one eternal Being, absolutely true and right and just, who made the world and its complex systems, its sound, light, colour, beauty and gave us our whole moral sense of right and wrong – that kind of devotion is beyond our ken. As for holiness, we know the word, but have no idea what it means.

David, however, did believe in such a God. He not only believed in him, but he experienced him and that experience compelled him to worship.

> Ascribe to the LORD, O mighty ones,
>   ascribe to the LORD glory and strength.
> Ascribe to the LORD the glory due to his name;
>   worship the LORD in the splendour of his holiness.
>   (Psalm 29:1–2)

> Among the gods there is none like you, O LORD;
>   no deeds can compare with yours.
> All the nations you have made
>   will come and worship before you, O LORD;
>   they will bring glory to your name.

> For you alone are great and do
>   marvellous deeds;
> you alone are God.
>
> (Psalm 86:8–10)

David worshipped God for his holiness, his justice, his love, his truth, his benign power, his steadfastness, his mercy and his majesty. He had, in one way or another, experienced all these sides of God's character and he wanted to pass that experience on to his people. He did this through the songs which he taught them to sing, through the singers and musicians which he trained and through the great temple which he designed and prepared and which was finally built by his son Solomon.

Prayer

There is some instinct in us which makes us pray to God when we are in trouble; but not all who pray in a crisis have the experience of a dialogue with God. That experience only comes, as it did with David, when we are prepared to listen to the voice of conscience which God has given to all mankind. Prayer sharpens conscience. It also, for those who want to hear God's point of view, reminds us of the law he has given us. Additionally, as our dialogue with God develops, we can see, in the unfolding of the events about which we have prayed, a divine response. In the course of time, pattern and consistency develop in that message so that we come to know the ways of God and how he applies his written word to our lives. There is no doubt in the minds of those who have prayed consistently over the years, as David did, that there is a God out there, and that as we pray, he responds. We discover a pattern in the response which is consistent with and reinforces the law which he has given us to guide us through this rough and wicked world.

> When I called, you answered me;
>   you made me bold and stout-hearted.
>
> (Psalm 138:3)

O LORD, you have searched me
　　and you know me.
You know when I sit and when I rise;
　　you perceive my thoughts from afar.
You discern my going out and my
　　lying down;
　　you are familiar with all my ways.
Before a word is on my tongue
　　you know it completely, O LORD.
You hem me in – behind and before;
　　you have laid your hand upon me.
　　　　　　　　　　　(Psalm 139:1–5)

I love the house where you live, O LORD,
　　the place where your glory dwells.
　　　　　　　　　　　　　(Psalm 26:8)

I will praise the LORD, who counsels me;
　　even at night my heart instructs me.
I have set the LORD always before me,
　　Because he is at my right hand
　　I shall not be shaken.
Therefore my heart is glad and my
　　tongue rejoices;
　　my body also will rest secure,
because you will not abandon me
　　to the grave,
　　nor will you let your Holy One see decay.
　　　　　　　　　　　(Psalm 16:7–10)

I call on you, O God, for you will
　　answer me,
　　give ear to me and hear my prayer.
Show the wonder of your great love,
　　you who save by your right hand
　　those who take refuge in you
　　from their foes.
　　　　　　　　　　　　(Psalm 17:6–7)

Humility

A person who walks with God cannot help but be humble. The greatness and majesty of God puts all else into perspective. God is eternal, we are just a passing shadow, here today and gone tomorrow. All the strength and talent we have come from the God who created us. God is holy and, the more we contrast ourselves with that holiness, the more we see all the flaws in our character, all the self-interest in our actions. When God honoured David with the great covenant which established his kingdom and dynasty, David asked who was he in God's sight and who was his father's house that he should have such an honour?

David knew that, without God's help, he would never have won the kingdom, beaten off its enemies, enlarged its borders or established peace and security. He knew later that he would never have survived Absalom's rebellion without God's protection. So he did not establish a magnificent court, surround himself with flatterers or raise a standing army and go out on a war of unprovoked aggression.

David's faults

We may still ask how David, with all his faults, could still be 'a man after God's own heart'. There were times when his faith failed. There were times when his sword seems to us to have cut too far. He took too many wives and not all of them shared his faith in God. Above all, there was his double crime of adultery and murder against Uriah the Hittite.

The answer must be that none of us is perfect. All that distinguishes us is our attitude to our faults. There are those who self-righteously deny or belittle them and there are those who see them for what they are and repent of them as David did. What brings us to understanding and repentance is the frame of mind that David had, especially his love for God, his honour and his law.

Every king who succeeded him was compared to David. The question was whether or not they 'walked in all the ways of David their father'. Very few came up to this strict standard.

Then, four centuries later, Jerusalem was captured, the temple destroyed and the princes and leaders killed or deported. Though the dynasty died, the eternal covenant lived on, pointing down the years ahead to great David's greater Son and a kingdom greater in scope, spirit and power than any ever known.

7
Great David's greater Son

The time when Israel was united under David and Solomon was a golden age to which the prophets looked back, urging the two kingdoms to return to the faith of David and to put away their idols.

Only in Judah were there kings whose faith and conduct could be compared to that of David – Asa, Jehoshaphat, Joash (until the death of Jehoiada the priest), Azariah, Hezekiah and Josiah. But even the best of them, bright lights though they were in that sea of darkness, could not compare to David.

Yet, through all the dire prophetic warnings of the disasters which were fulfilled in the conquest and exile of both Israel and Judah, shines a gleam of hope. God will always preserve a remnant of those who trust in him as David did; to that remnant will come a ruler from David's line whose kingdom will never fail. These prophecies pick up and spell out in more detail the covenant which God himself had made with David.

The central passages are in the prophecies of Isaiah and Jeremiah.

> A shoot will come up from
>   the stump of Jesse;
>   from his roots a Branch will bear fruit.
> The Spirit of the LORD will rest upon him –
>   the Spirit of widsom and of understanding,
>   the Spirit of counsel and of power,
>   the Spirit of knowledge and of the fear of
>   the LORD;
> and he will delight in the fear of the LORD.
>
> He will not judge by what he sees
>   with his eyes,
>   or decide by what he hears with his ears;
> but with righteousness he will judge the needy,

with justice he will give decisions
for the poor of the earth.

(Isaiah 11:1–4)

'The days are coming,' declares the LORD,
'when I will raise up to David a
righteous Branch,
a King who will reign wisely
and do what is just and right in the land.
In his days Judah will be saved
and Israel will live in safety.
This is the name by which he will be called:
The LORD Our Righteousness.'

(Jeremiah 23:5–6)

'In those days and at that time,
I will make a righteous Branch
sprout from David's line;
he will do what is just and right
in the land.
In those days Judah will be saved
and Jerusalem will live in safety.
This is the name by which he will be called:
The LORD Our Righteousness.'

(Jeremiah 33:15–16)

'I will place over them one shepherd, my servant
David, and he will tend them; he will tend them and
be their shepherd. I the LORD will be their God, and
my servant David will be prince among them. I the
LORD have spoken.'

(Ezekiel 34:23–24)

Jews and Christians not only share David as a part of our
joint Judaeo-Christian heritage, we also share all of the law and
the prophets, including the Psalms. So we believe together in
a Messiah descended from David, bringing salvation and ruling
with justice.

The founders of the Christian church, the twelve apostles, were all Jews who believed in the law and the prophets. Originally the Christian church was seen by others as a Jewish sect, called 'The Way'. The Christian account, the Acts of the Apostles, tells us that many of the Jewish leaders became members of the church and, in their sermons and letters, their argument that Jesus was the promised Messiah was closely reasoned from the words of Moses and the prophets.

They also declared, as a matter of fact to which the apostles were witnesses, that Jesus of Nazareth, who had been crucified by the order of the Roman governor, Pontius Pilate, had risen from the dead and had been seen by three hundred people. The body had been placed under armed Roman guard in a sealed tomb just in case such a claim were made. When the claim was made, however, no body was produced by the Romans or the Jewish leaders to refute it, so belief in the resurrection of Jesus grew. Since, under Jewish law, two witnesses were enough to establish a statement, the witness of twelve apostles and several hundred others, all in considerable danger when they spoke out, added to their credibility as witnesses and to the increasing number of Jews who joined them.

The five-fold argument of the apostles

The apostles, however, had also to show that their beliefs about Jesus and his teaching were the correct interpretation of the prophetic statements and that they fulfilled the law of Moses. Their initial statements come down to us in the Acts of the Apostles and their detailed arguments in the letters which they wrote to the churches. In addition, Matthew, the apostle, and Luke, who also wrote the Acts of the Apostles, both preface their accounts of the life of Jesus with a genealogical table, tracing his ancestry back to David. This was not an extraordinary achievement, since we know from the accounts of Ezra and Nehemiah of the care which the Jews took to maintain such records.

The main dispute, however, was not in the genealogies; it was differing in the interpretation of the prophets. Until then the hope of the Jewish people had been for a leader exactly like David, who would restore the political independence of the nation, throw out its foreign rulers and protect its worship. There was, of course, a great deal in the prophets which could not be fitted into this simple pattern, but we could well understand it if no-one wanted to complicate the simple faith which held the nation together while it was under the oppressive occupation. We can also understand the outrage and anger when the followers of Jesus argued from the prophecies themselves that the Messiah was to reign over a spiritual and not an earthly kingdom.

In the first place, they pointed out that the prophecies spoke of a never-ending reign, a king whom death could not hold and whose body would not see decay.

> Therefore my heart is glad and my
> tongue rejoices;
> my body will also rest secure,
> because you will not abandon me to the grave,
> nor will you let your Holy One
> see decay.
>
> (Psalm 16:9–10)

> The LORD has sworn
> and will not change his mind;
> You are a priest for ever,
> in the order of Melchizedek.
>
> (Psalm 110:4)

> Of the increase of his government
> and peace
> there will be no end.
> He will reign on David's throne
> and over his kingdom,
> establishing and upholding it
> with justice and righteousness
> from that time on and for ever.
>
> (Isaiah 9:7)

The apostles argued that these passages could not refer to a king who was mortal like David. They could and did refer to Jesus, however, who had risen from the dead and had ascended, in their sight, to be with God. They also pointed out that what happened to Jesus had not been done in a corner, but in Jerusalem during the Passover feast when the city was crowded. The apostles insisted that their account and those of the witnesses had been open to formal public challenge, but instead every effort had been made to keep them all quiet.

In the second place, the apostles pointed to the passages on the Messiah's relationship with God and with his fellow men, arguing that the Messiah was no mere human being.

> The LORD says to my Lord:
> 'Sit at my right hand
> until I make your enemies
> a footstool for your feet.'
> (Psalm 110:1)

It was generally accepted that 'The LORD' was God and that 'my Lord' whom he was addressing was the Messiah. Yet, though he was his offspring, David called him 'Lord' and God told this person to sit at his right hand, sharing a position of divine authority. For David to call his promised descendant 'Lord', he must consider him to be a higher order of being, since sons pay respect to their fathers and not the other way round. Furthermore, if he was to sit at God's right hand, he had to be the most exalted of beings.

Psalm 2 also tells of a father and son relationship,

> I will proclaim the decree of the Lord:
> He said to me, 'You are my Son;
>   today I have become your Father.
> Ask of me,
>   and I will make the nations your inheritance,
>   the ends of the earth your possession.'
> (Psalm 2:7–8)

The prophet Isaiah also has a passage showing that, though he is human, he is more than human.

> For to us a child is born,
>   to us a son is given,
>   and the government will be on
>   his shoulders.
> And he will be called
>   Wonderful, Counsellor, Mighty God,
>   Everlasting Father, Prince of peace.
>   (Isaiah 9:6)

All these passages are compatible with the Messiah as a king, which was the Jewish expectation, or they go beyond the position of an earthly king. But, just as his power went beyond that of a human king, so other passages seemed to show that, from a worldly point of view, he seemed something less than a king,

> He had no beauty or majesty to
>   attract us to him,
>   nothing in his appearance that
>   we should desire him.
> He was despised and rejected by men
>   a man of sorrows and familiar
>   with suffering.
> Like one from whom men must hide
>   their faces
>   he was despised and we
>   esteemed him not.
>
> Surely he took up our infirmities
>   and carried our sorrows,
> yet we considered him stricken by God,
>   smitten by him, and afflicted.
> But he was pierced for our
>   transgressions,
>   he was crushed for our iniquities;

the punishment that brought us
 peace was upon him,
 and by his wounds we are healed.
We all, like sheep, have gone astray,
 each of us has turned to his own way;
and the LORD has laid on him
 the iniquity of us all.

(Isaiah 53:2b–6)

The apostles themselves had the greatest difficulty in believing that the Messiah should suffer and die and, like a sacrificial lamb, bear the sins of the people. They had wanted Jesus to reign like a proper king and when he was crucified by the Romans and literally 'pierced', they all scattered.

Only when they had witnessed his resurrection and when he had shown them where the prophets had foretold the unavoidable and final sacrifice for sins, did they see that his death was part of the divine plan; it was not a disaster, on the contrary, it was the good news which he now wanted them to proclaim.

The good news was that, with the death of Jesus, there was no more need to offer sacrifice for sins. God was still just and rebellion against our Creator was punishable, but for all who renounced their rebellion and accepted God's offer of forgiveness, Christ's sacrifice was sufficient. He was the Son of David, through Mary, but had been conceived through the Spirit of God and did not inherit the sinful nature of his fathers. The Messiah was not a sinful man, but, like the first man Adam, had a nature which was not bound to sin.

So the salvation brought by the Messiah was of a far greater order than that which had been brought by David or which could have been brought by another king like David. A king might have thrown out the Romans as David threw out the Philistines. There might have been, for his life and that of his successor, another golden age. People might have come from other countries to Jerusalem to worship. But none of that would have dealt with the corruption deep in the human heart, the corruption which had made first Israel and then Judah forget

133

David, the law of Moses and the fear of God. Instead Jesus, the Messiah, had, through his death as a sacrifice for the sins of all who believed him, brought a reconciliation with God and an eternal kingdom from all peoples and nations.

In David's own words,

> Blessed is he
>   whose transgressions are
>   forgiven,
>   whose sins are covered.
> Blessed is the man
>   whose sins the LORD does not
>   count against him
> and in whose spirit is no deceit.
> (Psalm 32:1–2)

In the third place, the apostles argued that this salvation came by faith in the Messiah and not through the law of Moses. Many of the Jewish community resisted the idea of a Messianic sacrifice on the grounds that for those who kept the law of Moses, there was no need for such a sacrifice.

Others accepted the argument of the apostles that no-one was capable of keeping the law. They had weighty passages to back this argument, starting with the words of David.

> The LORD looks down from heaven
>   on the sons of men
> to see if there are any who
>   understand,
>   any who seek God.
> All have turned aside,
>   they have together become
>   corrupt;
> there is no-one who does good,
>   not even one.
> (Psalm 14:2–3)

134

> There is no fear of God
> before his eyes.
> (Psalm 36:1)

> Who has believed our message
> and to whom has the arm of the LORD
> been revealed?
> (Isaiah 53:1)

> Their feet rush into sin;
> they are swift to shed innocent blood.
> Their thoughts are evil thoughts,
> ruin and destruction mark their ways.
> The way of peace they do not know;
> there is no justice in their paths
> They have turned them into
> crooked roads;
> no-one who walks in them will
> know peace.
> (Isaiah 59:7–8)

These were criticisms by Israel's greatest king and greatest prophet of those who had the law and so, the apostles argued, trying to keep the law was not enough to save us from God's justice.

They pointed out that God had made promises to those who had lived before the law was ever given and that he had blessed them for their faith in those promises. So it was faith which had saved the patriarchs from whom Israel was descended, Abraham, Isaac, Jacob and all the others who had acted in faith on God's promises. The apostolic but anonymous Letter to the Hebrews lists those in the sacred Jewish writings of whom it could be said,

> These were all commended for their faith, yet none of them received what had been promised. God had planned something better for us so that only together with us would they be made perfect (Hebrews 11:39).

135

The writer listed Abel, Enoch, Noah, Abraham, Isaac, Jacob, Joseph, Moses' parents, Moses himself, the prostitute Rahab, Gideon, Barak, Samson, Jephthah, David, Samuel and all the prophets.

The law, argued the apostles, was not there to make us perfect, but to make us realize how imperfect we were and how much we needed to be saved from God's justice against those who broke his law. Those who believed his promises that he would provide a way of salvation, had been saved by their faith in the promise. We who know of the fulfilment of the promise were saved by our faith in the Messiah who had died as our once for all and eternal sacrifice.

One of the fiercest opponents of this point of view was a Jewish intellectual of the strict sect of the Pharisees and he did his best to put down the new heresy. But in the end, while going to Damascus to imprison those Jews who held this heresy, Paul was confronted by Jesus – the last to see him – and was converted. He then put his great intellect at the service of those Jews who believed that Jesus was the Messiah, the sacrifice for sins and our continuing High Priest.

In the fourth place, the apostles pointed to the promises of a new covenant between God and man.

> And afterwards,
>   I will pour out my Spirit on all people.
> Your sons and daughters will prophesy,
>   your old men will dream dreams,
>   your young men will see visions.
> Even on my servants, both men and women,
>   I will pour out my Spirit in those days.
>   (Joel 2:28, 29, 32a)

> 'The time is coming,' declares the LORD,
>   'when I will make a new covenant
> with the house of Israel
>   and with the house of Judah.
> It will not be like the covenant
>   I made with their forefathers

when I took them by the hand
  to lead them out of Egypt,
because they broke my covenant,
  though I was a husband to them,'
                    declares the LORD.
'This is the covenant that I will
    make with the house of Israel
  after that time,' declares the LORD.
'I will put my law in their minds
  and write it on their hearts.
I will be their God,
  and they will be my people.
No longer will a man teach his neighbour,
  or a man his brother, saying,
    ''Know the LORD,''
because they will all know me,
  from the least of them to the
    greatest,'
                    declares the LORD.
'For I will forgive their wickedness
  and will remember their sins no more.'
                   (Jeremiah 31:31–34)

Just as the Spirit of God came on David, so the apostles
found that the Spirit of God came on them and turned them
from a frightened group, meeting behind barred doors, to a
courageous group. So they went out, as David had done, to
preach the good news and stood up to those opponents who
had the power to imprison or execute them.

Through the centuries those who followed the apostles'
teaching have found this indwelling spirit, sharpening our
conscience into an acute sense of right and wrong, and
increasingly giving us the power (which we had lacked without
it) of doing what is right, avoiding what is wrong and, where
we have not avoided it, of coming to God, as David did, in
repentance.

Perhaps the strongest evidence we have, that the spirit which
came on David is the same spirit which has come on us, is the

love we Christians have for his psalms. There is no feeling which he expresses which we do not find in ourselves, and there is little that we find in ourselves which he does not express far better than we could ever do. That is why three thousand years later we still pray his prayers and sing his songs.

In the fifth place, and most controversial of all, the apostles came slowly to accept – but having accepted to teach without further doubt – that the new covenant was no longer confined to Israel, but extended to all the peoples of the world.

This was the one part of their teaching which was most unacceptable to their contemporary Jewish leaders because the separation of Israel from the surrounding nations had been taught so firmly and for so long. Israel had to distance itself from the idolatry practised on all sides. Inter-marriage was absolutely forbidden and so was social intercourse. Otherwise the truth contained in the law and the prophets, passed on intact from generation to generation of faithful Jews, would become polluted by the idolatry of the Gentiles. During the times of the kings, Israel had kept on falling into the idolatry of the surrounding races. Since the end of the Babylonian captivity, however, their worship had been kept pure.

Yet, in the very law and prophets which they were protecting, there were promises to the Gentiles. They were to be found even in God's covenant with Abraham.

> . . . all peoples on earth
> will be blessed through you.
> (Genesis 12:3b)

Abraham will surely become a great and powerful nation, and all nations on earth will be blessed through him (Genesis 18:18).

. . . through your offspring [singular, referring to one person] all nations on earth will be blessed, because you have obeyed me (Genesis 22:18).

Moses himself, in a song which forecasts Israel's rebellion against their God, says

> I will make them envious by those
> who are not a people;
> I will make them angry by a
> nation that has no understanding.
> (Deuteronomy 32:21b)

David himself refers to the other nations,

> Therefore I will praise you, O LORD,
> among the nations;
> I will sing praises to your name.
> (2 Samuel 22:50)

Another psalm, not attributed to David, adds,

> Praise the LORD, all you nations;
> extol him, all you peoples.
> (Psalm 117:1)

Isaiah is more specific.

In that day the Root of Jesse will stand as a banner for the peoples; the nations will rally to him, and his place of rest will be glorious (Isaiah 11:10).

> I will also make you a light for the Gentiles,
> that you may bring my salvation
> to the ends of the earth.
> (Isaiah 49:6b)

> I revealed myself to those who did not ask for me;
> I was found by those who did not seek me.
> To a nation that did not call on my name,
> I said 'Here am I, here am I'.
> (Isaiah 65:1)

Hosea is also more specific,

> I will say to those called 'Not
>   my people', 'You are my people',
> and they will say, 'You are my God'.
>   (Hosea 2:23b)

The apostles taught that the key function of the Jewish nation had been to keep the law and the prophets secure and to bear witness to the one God, Maker of heaven and earth, until the new covenant was introduced by the Messiah from David's line. Then the Spirit of God would come on all who trusted in him, both Jew and Gentile and God's spiritual kingdom would stretch out from the Jews to all the peoples whom God created and to whom he now offered a place in his kingdom.

Not all Israel would come into this spiritual kingdom. But then not all those who had descended from Abraham, Isaac and Jacob had been obedient to the law. Indeed those who had been faithful were usually only a remnant of the whole nation. Because of the promises, however, God would preserve Israel as a people and in the end, when the good news had reached out to all the Gentiles, Israel would be re-grafted into the true vine. Then, according to the Apostle Paul,

> Israel has experienced a hardening in part until the full
> number of the Gentiles has come in. And so all Israel
> will be saved, as it is written:
>
> 'The deliverer will come from Zion;
>   he will turn godlessness away from Jacob.
> And this is my covenant with them
>   when I take away their sins.'
> (Letter to the Romans: 11:25b, 26–27a, quoting Isaiah
> 59:20–21; 27:9).

It would be presumptuous for a Christian to try to give, even in outline, the present view of the Jewish people on the coming

GREAT DAVID'S GREATER SON

of the Messiah. It is remarkable that, nearly two thousand years after the destruction of Jerusalem by the Roman Emperor Titus and their dispersion across the Empire, there remains a Jewish race, still held together in worship. Where, today, are the Philistines, the Assyrians, the Babylonians? Where are the later races like the Carthaginians? Where are the races which overthrew the great Roman Empire, the Goths, the Vandals, the Visigoths? The great Mongol Empire has also long since disappeared. Yet, in this kaleidoscope of peoples, the scattered Jewish people have remained intact. They have survived even the horror of Hitler's holocaust. There can be no doubt that they are still a special people.

8

A commentary for Christians

Faith

David's life has always been a source of inspiration to Christians. As we read the Psalms, we share his very human fears, hopes, prayers and are at the same time uplifted by his faith. When we are tempted and sin, we are helped by his prayers of repentance, but above all it is his strong and simple faith in God which strengthens our faith, too.

There must have been many courageous men in Israel, but only David had the faith to go out to fight Goliath. An even greater test of his faith came when King Saul turned against him through jealousy, tried to kill him and then hunted him through the wild desert country south of Judah.

David had the faith, even after Saul's death, to wait for God's time before he went up to Judah. Furthermore, he waited for over seven years until the other clans came to ask him to reign over them too.

When he was king, David waited for God's call before going out to fight, but when the call came he went at once, whatever the odds against him.

But even David's great faith could fail. Twice he went to the Philistines, despairing of God's capacity to keep him safe, and after all his victories, achieved without conscription, he went so far as to forget what God had done that he made a roll of all the fighting men of Israel.

That must warn us that the exercise of faith is no guarantee against doubt, which can strike when we are least expecting it and can lead us dangerously astray. But with all his failings, we can learn a great deal from David's faith, both in what he did and in the reasons he gives in the psalms for his faith.

David trusted God's law, given by Moses and written in his conscience, against all the arguments of self-interest, self-preservation, worldly wisdom, pride and prudence, which move those around us and which tempt us to forget what God has said.

Faith believes that there is one God, who gave us life, who, in his love, gave us his law to guide us through this uncertain world. Faith trusts that God's law and his ways are good, that to keep them honours him whatever risk to ourselves, but that whatever happens, the Lord loves us, cares for us and will keep his promises.

Faith makes those who have it reliable and predictable in a world of uncertain and unreliable relationships. Our friends, our family, our colleagues, all know where they are with us. It injects firm foundations into the shifting sands of society. But above all a firm faith means that God can rely on us, as he relied on David.

Private prayer

David was a man of prayer. His relationship with the great God, who had made the universe, was person to person. We are told that, from the time that Samuel anointed him, God's Spirit came upon him. We believe as Christians that when we ask God's forgiveness for our sins through the atoning work of Jesus Christ, the Spirit comes on us too – as it did on the early disciples. That is why, like David, we want to pray, to tell God that we trust him, that we love him, that we want to do his will and then, like David, tell him what worries us and ask him for his help.

Prayer divides formal religion from true faith. There is nothing formal in David's prayers. They are not mechanical, like prayer beads or a prayer wheel. They are the communication of a person made in the image of God to the God who made us all different, knows us individually and has promised to hear and answer those who trust him.

And God does answer prayer. Those who have prayed year after year, decade after decade, get to know how God answers prayer. He reminds us of what he has said through the law, the prophets and the apostles. Passages we had forgotten come clearly to our minds. He talks to us through our consciences. What we had wanted to do appears to us in its real, mean, selfish light. What he wants us to do appears to us as the duty it always was, but which we wanted to forget. As we thank him for answering past prayers, like specific requests which, against all the human odds, have been granted, our faith is reinforced and we are encouraged to continue to put to him all our burdens for others as well as for ourselves. Furthermore, we find that the prayers, the private worship, and the thanksgiving of David, put in words all that we are feeling and thinking.

God does not give us all we want. The first child born to David and Bathsheba became ill. In anguish David pleaded with God for its recovery and would not eat. The child, however, died. His servants were afraid to tell David in case he did something desperate. But the king said that while the child was alive he had fasted and wept, saying 'Who knows, the Lord may be gracious to me and let the child live.' Now that he knew the answer, David went about his business.

It is not easy for us to accept a negative answer to our prayers as David did. But if we really believe that God hears us and loves us, then we should. He has not told us that he will exempt us from sickness and death and all the other results of human rebellion against God. Christ prayed before the crucifixion that if it was the Father's will, this cup might pass from him. 'Nevertheless,' he continued, 'not my will, but yours be done.'

David asked God for guidance and had the priest to give him the answer. We do not have a priest to tell us whether to go up to battle or not. Christ and the apostles, however, have spelt out God's law much more explicitly than the Old Testament prophets. They have given us moral duties and obligations to others which are our guidelines when we wonder what to do. We find that we cannot pray without becoming acutely conscious of our duties and obligations. Members of Parliaments have a strong primary obligation to those who elect them, so that is the fundamental test in any dilemma on political action. If we think these obligations have become intolerable, then we need to make the strongest possible objective check. David went on obeying his king at peril of his life. Yet even when he had escaped from men Saul had sent to kill him, he made one final check with Jonathan, who was both his friend and the king's son. Until then Jonathan had continued to reassure him and to reason with Saul. If Jonathan finally believed that Saul wanted to murder David without trial and could not be restrained and advised David to fly for his life, then and only then would his obligation end.

Over time a pattern develops in our dialogue with God. David, as an outlaw, prayed to be rescued from those who were chasing him. Time and again God answered his prayer. That gave David the confidence that Samuel had not anointed him for nothing and that God would deal with Saul. Then suddenly his faith cracked and, out of character, he despaired, did not pray to God, but set out for the Philistine king of Gath with his faithful band. We need to recognize the pattern of prayer and answer, because it will hold us when times get tough and our faith is tried. It was not the end. David was forced to turn to God again and his faith returned in full force. Prayer is not easy. But when we read David's prayers, we find it easier.

Public worship

It is probably not too much to say that David invented public worship. Moses laid down the details of sacrifices, but these were performed by the priests and the public were kept at a distance. David's public worship involved everyone.

There were the psalms, which he composed for all to sing. The psalms contained great truths about God in rhythmic cadence and, as the people repeated them or sang them together, they stuck in the memory. Congregations have been repeating or singing psalms ever since.

The psalms which David composed and those which were added to complete, over generations, the whole book of one hundred and fifty psalms, were set in the life of his day. Since then, too, Christians want to sing about the work of Christ and the power of the Holy Spirit, so a whole new range of subjects have been added. As the world changes, so the styles and settings change and the hymns change too. But the principle of expressing spiritual truth in song has not changed.

There are a good many songs sung in churches today which

do not express spiritual truth, but are more in the nature of a 'mantra', a repetitious slogan, which might, with a slight change of words, be sung by any religion. The repetitive singing may work the singers into an ecstasy that has more to do with psychology than with the expression of a reasoning faith. We need to use our singing as David did, to worship God. Reason reinforces emotion; it does not destroy it. Singing the truth keeps it in our hearts and minds for the moment when we are tried and tempted and need it in a hurry. There is more to the Christian faith than the repetition of slogans and, since we have great hymns, it is a pity to settle for less. Furthermore, we should sing in a language which we understand.

David added to his psalms the music of his day, harps, lyres, tambourines, cymbals, ram's horns and trumpets. Of the descendants of Aseph there were, according to the Chronicles, close on three hundred people 'trained and skilled in music for the LORD, young and old, teacher as well as student' (1 Chronicles 25:5) who took their duty turns.

There is a lot of unnecessary argument about music in churches. Some refuse to have any instruments at all. Some will have a piano, but not an organ, some draw the line at saxophones, and some at drums. David seems to have used all the instruments available to him. But if, for instance, Africans find that drums remind them too much of pagan ritual or if the saxophone reminds those in other countries too much of jazz bands, they should not be imposed. We want all to be able to worship together in harmony of spirit as well as voice.

It is also a good rule that the music should be the servant of the words, should enhance them and make them easier to remember. We can hardly believe that David the psalmist allowed the music to obliterate the words or to allow the words to be subsidiary to the operatic voice. Choirs, therefore, should help the singing; they should not dominate it.

David teaches us, in this way, that God gave the gifts of poetry and music and we should use them to worship him and to glorify him.

We also read that, when bringing the ark back to Jerusalem,

David, wearing a linen ephod instead of his royal robes, danced before the Lord. There are those who believe that this justifies dance in church worship. Miriam, Moses' sister, had also danced with the women after the great crossing of the Red Sea. It is argued, on the other hand, that these were both quite outstanding occasions and that dancing had sexual associations in those days as it does today, which confined it to spontaneous expression at exceptional celebrations. They also point out that we never find dancing in the New Testament. Let the last two psalms have the last word.

> Let Israel rejoice in their Maker;
>   let the people of Zion be glad in
>   their King.
> Let them praise his name with dancing
>   and make music to him with
>   tambourine and harp.
> (Psalm 149:2–3)

> Praise him with the sounding of the trumpet,
>   praise him with the harp and lyre,
> praise him with tambourine and dancing,
>   praise him with the strings and flute.
> (Psalm 150:3–4)

David also made public prayers on the return of the ark and on receiving gifts for the temple, which are a model of praise and worship, in which the people could join in their hearts and give their spoken assent at the end. 'Then all the people said "Amen" and "Praise the LORD" ' (1 Chronicles 16:36b). 'Then David said to the whole assembly, "Praise the LORD your God." So they all praised the LORD the God of their fathers' (1 Chronicles 29:20a).

David's prayers were an acknowledgment of the greatness and glory of God, and of the gratitude of his people and a plea to God on behalf of the people that he would keep them.

There are those who believe that public prayer to God should be dignified and formal and others who believe that it should be spontaneous. Ideally it should be both spontaneous and worthy as David's was, but we are human and this is not easy. Most churches now have a mixture of the two kinds and maybe that is best. Certainly spontaneous public prayer tests the spiritual strength of those who offer it, and puts a burden on the congregation if the spiritual strength is not there – or if expressions of opinion take over, as in the story where, after fifteen minutes, the small boy in the front row piped up 'Open your eyes, man, you're preaching.'

Whether formal or spontaneous, all who pray in public would do well to set their standard by David's public prayers and by his psalms that can act as a model for public prayers.

The Chronicles show that David took great care that public worship should be to the glory of God. He organized the Levites 'to help Aaron's descendants in the service of the temple of the LORD . . . they were to stand every morning to thank and praise the Lord. They were to do the same every evening . . . and at appointed feasts' (1 Chronicles 23:28, 30–31). He organized the singers, he set aside Levites to supervise the building of the temple, made plans for the temple and raised the money to build it. The early church met in houses. The Lord has promised, 'Where two or three come together in my name, there I am with them' (Matthew 18:19).

As the church grew, so did the buildings – fine churches, like the fourth-century churches of San Vitale, Ravenna. By the twelfth and thirteenth century the church dominated society and Europe built its great cathedrals, culminating in the most extravagant of all, St Peter's in Rome, which was financed by the sale of indulgences. The question is whether these cathedrals were to the glory of God or to human glory. By comparison, the temple designed by David was a relatively simple building, though the fittings were of the finest.

Perhaps the best message that David can leave us is that worship should be to the glory of God and not to human glory. John Laing, the builder, was a Plymouth Brother and they believed in simple buildings for their basic form of worship. However, he put his very best craftsmen to build the 'Gospel Hall' at Burnt Oak in North London, where he himself worshipped. That was his way of honouring God in the tradition of David and that simple hall, superbly built, still stands to the glory of God.

Leader

In our democratic age we are suspicious of leaders. We prefer synods and general assemblies over which Archbishops and Moderators warily preside. But leadership does not come with high office. Leadership has to be earned and democracy tries to see that it is. That is also a Christian principle. Our Lord has told us, 'If anyone wants to be first, he must be the very last, and the servant of all' (Mark 9:35), and 'I am among you as one who serves' (Luke 22:27b).

It was also David's way. He earned his leadership through service to his king and country, to his fellow outlaws, through patience in building a united country and in defending it against its enemies on all sides. When he stayed comfortably at home during the siege of Rabbah, he set in train a series of events which nearly cost him his crown, despite all his previous service.

A true leader accepts responsibility when no-one else will dare. David was so outraged by Goliath that he accepted the responsibility of fighting him and all the risk which went with it. When Saul sent him against the Philistines, hoping that they would kill him, David accepted it cheerfully, leading his troops into battle. When he became an outlaw, he took responsibility for his father and mother, sending them over to safety in Moab. When the outcasts of society joined him, he accepted responsibility for all of them, for their safety and their food. They in turn followed him because he cared for them and risked his life for theirs.

The Christian church needs leaders who accept inconvenient responsibility for the flock, who are less concerned for their reputation in worldly society and more concerned to defend the faith, less concerned with positions and more concerned with service.

A leader trusts in God and inspires followers to do the same. With rare exceptions, David moved as an outlaw as the Lord told him to move. He clearly passed his faith in God to the others and they moved with him. It was a terrible time, a time of betrayal by those who wanted the king's favour, a time when the king's forces seemed so near and when David's men were hemmed in between the desert and their enemies. Yet the band held together – there were no desertions – moved together, and fought together.

Twice David refused to remove the central problem confronting him by killing Saul and his band respected his judgment. Only after the Amalakites took their families in a raid on Keilah did they come near to turning on him. He had not asked God about going to the Philistines. But it was David's leadership through mutual commitment in common danger which welded them together and his example of leadership gave him a team of leaders, tried by fire, to serve the nation for the next forty years.

It is one matter to lead six hundred. It is quite another to lead a nation, but David made the transition. He gradually built a consensus, starting with Judah, making gestures of friendship to those who rescued the bodies of Saul and Jonathan, refusing to press his advantage against Abner until finally the other clans came to him and asked him to be king over them too. After Absalom's rebellion, he was careful to build the consensus again, involving Amasa, who had led Absalom's forces. Joab, who did not believe in consensus, killed Abner and Amasa, for which David never forgave him. In Joab's way lay bitterness, revenge and perpetual feud. In David's way lay the long peace of the golden years.

There are those, even among Christians, who do not believe in consensus. Christians, particularly those who believe that they have God on their side in every detail, are especially against consensus. Oliver Cromwell told the Scots Presbyterians, 'I pray you brethren, in the bowels of Christ, consider whether ye be not mistaken.' It was Cromwell, too, who allowed Jews to settle again in England. He did not agree with their doctrine, but they had every right to hold it. To respect another's point of view does not mean that we share it. Toleration is not a lowest common denominator of belief.

What we tolerate is the right of others to be wrong.

Politically, too, there are those who do not believe in consensus. They believe that their creed is right, that it should be taken to its full and logical conclusion so long as they have constitutional power to enforce it. Others believe that nothing is finally settled that way. Laws passed by one government without consensus are immediately repealed by its opponents as soon as they gain power. Building a broad consensus is more tedious, more difficult, and involves compromises with what we would really like. Once gained, however, it is far more lasting and provides a more predictable legal base on which society can rest the millions of decisions and commitments people have to make. Governments should serve all the people, not just their own party.

Rulers who are by nature strong and powerful, should be especially careful to serve the weak. David had a particular care for the powerless and all who were dependent on just laws and just administration of those laws. The laws of Moses were egalitarian. Every fifty years, at the Jubilee, debts had to be cancelled, sequestered land had to be returned, slaves had to be set free. Otherwise the rich would get richer and the poor poorer. David came from an old family but not from a rich one. The youngest son, not a servant, looked after the sheep. He knew how it felt to be poor. He had been an outlaw. He knew how it felt to suffer injustice, to be oppressed.

Christians should have a special care for the poor. Of course work has to be rewarded. 'You shall not muzzle the ox which treads out the corn' (Deuteronomy 25:4) was an instruction of Moses applied by the Apostle Paul to human relations (1 Corinthians 9:9; 1 Timothy 5:18). But the rich should not monopolize wealth, adding home to home and field to field (Isaiah 5:8). The psalms of David are heavy with criticism of rich oppressors and of the needs of those who have no-one to help them.

Even in an affluent society, the poor can get poorer as the rich get richer. We should be governed by moral principles, not by economic dogmatism. If housing policy results in the break up of village communities, because none of the young

151

can get a house there, then there is something wrong with housing policy. If monetary and credit policy result in a sharp rise in personal debt and repossession of homes, then there is something the matter with monetary and credit policy. If those who run an industry need salaries ten times as high as those of cabinet ministers, then we need to turn back to a more egalitarian society.

David had another great quality of leadership; he admitted error. Too many leaders today believe that the cardinal sin is to admit to a mistake. As a result those mistakes are compounded and whatever remains under the obstinate leader's control goes from bad to worse. The stronger the leader, the more damage is done. David was not free from sin, but as soon as he saw his error, he repented fully and freely. He could not put everything right again, as we have seen, but the error was not compounded.

Error does not always arise from sin. We are all fallible and in this uncertain world all make misjudgments. The best political systems are those which allow the fastest and most sensitive feedback, leading to adjustment before too much damage is done. That is why democracy is a more effective system than autocracy, why societies need a free press, despite its abuse, and why autocracy runs blindly into the most terrible errors about which no-one dares to tell their rulers. That is why in churches we need elders who are prepared to listen, to admit mistakes, to apologize when necessary, and to put right what has gone wrong. That is why the pride and obstinacy which will not admit mistakes is such a bane to good leadership, why humility and the spirit of service to those under the leaders' care is such a help.

'Where there is no vision the people perish' (Proverbs 29:18). David was a leader of vision. He had a vision of Israel's God, the one true God, Maker of heaven and earth, awesome, holy, just; yet loving, personal, forgiving to all those who asked for forgiveness. He had a vision of Israel, God's chosen nation, a witness to the world around. He had a vision of the way in which God should be worshipped, the need for justice in the divinely anointed king, and the standard of behaviour which was fitting for God's own people.

Not only did David have this vision, he was able to communicate it. He could put into memorable verse and popular song the great truths about God, so that the people could sing them and remember them. He made Jerusalem the centre of worship for the whole kingdom, bringing the ark there, with a great and memorable public gathering. He set up the Tent of Meeting, organized the Levites and the feasts Moses had ordained, and prepared plans for the great temple. When he defeated the Philistines, he burnt their idols. We hear of no idolatry in Israel under David.

It is not enough for a leader to be an administrator, a decision-maker. They must be able to motivate, to engage the energy and talents of their generation in a cause which they believe to be worth fighting for, in goals which they are committed to achieving. They need to be able to inspire trust in their own integrity and in the integrity of the vision they give.

Although the world is full of false prophets with distorted visions, there is a great deal going for courageous Christian leadership and the vision they have to give. The Christian faith did not spread across the Roman Empire and then the world by accident. Its vision rang true to the human conscience, to people's perception of good and evil. Its vision of a life beyond death rang true to our feeling that death is more than the dropping of an autumn leaf, that it is a tragedy and that there must be a better life beyond. Its insistence on the punishment of evil and the reward of good rings true to our sense of justice. The Christian faith touches the guilt we all feel and our anxiety to atone and to relieve the burden of guilt. Its 'good news' is that the God who made us has given his Son to bear the burden of our guilt, and made a way of eternal reconciliation between the rebellious creature and a just Creator. Above all it is this 'good news' that has given a hope which no false prophet could conceive or match.

The twentieth century has seen a failure of Christian leadership on a grand scale as position after position was conceded to the false prophets by the official leaders of our churches. The vision and hope we have to give has been blunted as the church has accommodated the intellectual leaders of worldly opinion. David's vision and courage must be an inspiration to us and our leaders to give the vision which has been passed on to us by faithful men and women and which we must pass on in our turn in its full brilliance.

We can also learn from David's mistakes.

Marriage

From his time as an outlaw David had one moral weakness. He was a polygamist. He was originally married to Michal, second daughter of King Saul, but when David became an outlaw, Saul gave Michal in marriage to someone else. David still regarded her as his wife and, when negotiating for the accession of the northern clans to his kingdom, he made her return a condition of their good faith.

Yet, while an outlaw, he married a second wife, Ahinoam of Jezreel, mother of Amnon. We can sympathize with a young man in his twenties wanting a wife and seeing the sword of Saul and her second husband between him and his legitimate wife. He might have divorced Michal quite legally, but she had loved him and saved his life and his subsequent demand for her return was probably his personal desire, not just the re-establishing of a dynastic link. Then came his encounter with Abigail, a woman of great wisdom, tact and courage. When her husband had a stroke and died, David asked her to marry him.

Had David waited on God, instead of marrying Ahinoam – the behaviour of whose son does not say much for the mother – he might have settled for Abigail as his sole wife. Her continued presence at his side and their joint authority in a royal family in which they were both parents of all the children could have saved David from the divided and rebellious family which plagued his old age.

Moses' account of our first parents said that marriage was for companionship. Our Lord was opposed to divorce; when he was asked why Moses had allowed it he said that it was for the hardness of their hearts, but 'from the beginning it was not so'. Moses had also forbidden Israel's future kings to take

154

many wives, but when David became King of Hebron, this is exactly what he proceeded to do.

Polygamy turns an equal companionship between husband and wife into a rivalry between wives for the favours of the husband. When children come, the rivalry extends downwards to squabbles between the children of the different wives. The first account we have of such division is that of Abraham's family. His failure of faith in God's promise that God would give him a son and heir led to his having, at Sarah's suggestion, a son by Hagar, the handmaid of his wife Sarah. Then Sarah did have a son, and as he grew up there was rivalry between Ishmael, Hagar's son, and Isaac, Sarah's son. Sarah remained the only wife and she insisted that Hagar and Ishmael should leave. Isaac's marriage to Rebekah was not flawed by rivalry, but their son Jacob was tricked into marrying the elder daughter, Leah, when he had been betrothed to the younger Rachel and he ended up with two wives and two concubines. The rivalry there led to the older brothers conspiring against Rachel's son, Joseph, and selling him to slave traders on their way to Egypt.

All this would have been known to David. He must also have known that the prophet Samuel's father had taken a second wife and that the taunts of her rival had caused great grief to Samuel's mother until he was born. Yet in a society where monogamy was the rule and the general practice David took many wives.

The result was disastrous. The companionship of marriage was absent, which enables both partners, secure in each other's love and respect, to share their joys and troubles, which creates, over time, the trust in which loving advice can be given without fear and received without offence. At the end of his life even Bathsheba comes to ask a favour as a courtier to the king rather than as a wife to a husband and she was almost too late to tell the isolated monarch of the plot which was brewing.

The psalms also reflect David's agonizing isolation, when he could not trust even his friends. The companionship given by a good marriage to a faithful partner, who shares all our thoughts and anxieties, provides a stable element in an unstable world. Those who are without it may not realize what they miss.

David might have committed adultery even if he had only been married to one wife. It happens even among those who have David's faith. But, at the very least, one good wife makes it harder. Adding one to a number of wives is a matter of degree. Betraying the other partner and companion in a unique life-long relationship is much more difficult. You know each other so well that a shadow falls before anything irrevocable is done and a wise and loving spouse may win a partner back. Even before he was in trouble, David might have been persuaded that he should have been with the army and not at home.

In western societies, polygamy is illegal. But we have divorce 'at will', and what Muslims call 'serial polygamy'. They say that they can only have four wives, but we can have as many as we like, so long as we have them one at a time. So although we do not have rivalry in the same household, instead we have wives who are afraid to disagree with their husbands in case they walk out and take another woman. We have a sharp increase in the number of wives who have been left to bring up families single handed and while trying to earn enough to keep them at the same time – with a much smaller number of husbands trying to do the same. We have a sharp increase in step-fathers, many substituting well for a father who has gone, but many who feel no responsibility to disturbed step-children whom an increasing minority ill-treat and abuse.

Above all, divorce at will has introduced a destabilizing uncertainty into a relationship which, in Christian teaching, and loving social tradition, has been the strong stabilizing force in society. In civil disturbance, in war and famine, the state may have failed in the past, but at a much more basic level, the nuclear family and wider family held society together. There is nothing to assure us that the present social experiment will succeed and a great deal to tell us of the damage already done. Churches, who have to deal with the trauma of broken marriages and with young people, half of whom now come from broken homes, know how dangerously fragile our social structure has become. Indeed some are proposing that, regardless of the state's permissiveness, marriage in church should revert to the old commitments of marriage.

Temptation

When we contrast David's life up to the point of his adultery with Bathsheba, we must wonder at the ferocity of the temptation which wrecked David's reputation, undermined his moral leadership of the nation, lost him the respect of its leaders and his own family, and finally led to open rebellion by a favourite son. There are some lessons there on the nature of temptation and our reaction to it.

Firstly, if David could be tempted and fall, it shows that none of us, however strong our faith, is immune to temptation. Indeed our Lord himself was tempted and, though he did not fall, he needed care afterwards, so shattered was he by the experience. The Apostle Peter tells us 'Your enemy, the devil, prowls around like a roaring lion looking for someone to devour' (1 Peter 5:8). The Apostle Paul adds that, to resist the evil one, we must put on the full armour of God, 'the belt of truth buckled round your waist, with the breastplate of righteousness in place, and with your feet fitted with the readiness that comes from the gospel of peace . . . the shield of faith . . the helmet of salvation and the sword of the Spirit, which is the word of God' (Ephesians 6:14–17). The more prominent the leader, the more subject to spiritual warfare, the more necessary this spiritual discipline. Half-truth, half-righteous, half-faith, partial salvation and a blunted sword of the spirit leave us vulnerable as David was. The Christian faith is a full-time occupation and a full-time commitment.

Secondly, 'The devil finds work for idle hands to do.' Had David been doing his duty, he would not have been tempted to adultery with Bathsheba. We have more leisure today than ever before and more time to get into trouble. No-one works well when exhausted and we all need rest and those whose work demands mental concentration are in especial need of recreation. But Christians, called to be the salt of the earth and the light of the world, need to be disciplined, sober and careful in a society at play. While we have the strength, duty calls. David should have been with the soldiers in the field and not with the women at home.

Thirdly, while sexual sins are not the only sins, they are especially damaging. They damage and disrupt the closest, finest and highest human relationship, between a husband and wife, so they tear apart the closest of bonds. God made man and wife 'one flesh' and flesh cannot be torn apart without acute pain and mental trauma. They also damage the natural respect which most children show to good parents and split apart the family, that secure base where children should learn in an atmosphere of loving discipline. Whatever we may be told about a more permissive society, they do damage in the eyes of all who find out about them and in the case of leaders of society that damage can be terminal. In the case of church leaders it is terminal.

Fourthly, temptations of passion need, in the first instance, a cooling-off period. The heat of passion can cool, times of danger can pass. All the old disciplines of society aimed to give time to cool passions. If passions were not cooled, then there would be illegitimate children and the daughters who bore them found it harder to find a steady husband. With contraception and then the pill, these primary problems are not so acute and society has dropped its guard. Today our young people swim in a sea of sexual seduction and parents are borne along with the tide.

The laws of nature, however, have not been suspended. David's passion led directly to Amnon's incest with Tamar, and to Absalom's murder of Amnon and rebellion. Passion ends in tears, in jealousy and violence, in clinical depression, in unstable liaisons, in unhappy marriages, in divorce and in loneliness. The children of passion are today's mixed-up kids and tomorrow's unloved and violent teenagers. Some day the disciplines of society will return and meantime Christian families need, in love, to do the best they can.

Repentance and forgiveness

David, the sensitive poet, deeply conscious of the holiness of God and his justice, managed for a while to block out his moral sense. It can happen. Adultery also creates 'one flesh' and new obligations. In the excitement and new commitment all seems justified. But as soon as Nathan showed David his sin in its true light, his repentance was total, deep and genuine. He had offended against Uriah and Bathsheba, but above all he had offended against the laws of the God he loved. God forgave him. The child of the adulterous act did not survive, but God showed his forgiveness by giving David and Bathsheba another son, Solomon, who was to be his successor and through whom, eventually, the Messiah would come.

David was forgiven not by any formal penance, but by faith in the God he loved. The sin was a terrible aberration in the life of a good and godly man. But David believed that, through the Messiah, a way would be found to atone for sin and to redeem the sinner, and that faith saved him.

Faith did not save him from the human consequences of his sins. Those came thick and fast. But it re-established his relationship with God, it saved him eternally and he remained 'a man after God's own heart'.

Main biblical sources

Chapter 1: David and Goliath
1 Samuel 13–20.

Chapter 2: Outlaw
1 Samuel 21–28.

Chapter 3: King
2 Samuel 1–8, 10.

Chapter 4: Trouble
2 Samuel 9, 11–24.

Chapter 5: Rebellion and crisis
1 Kings 1–2;
1 Chronicles 17, 22, 25, 28, 29.